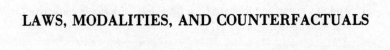

LAWS, MODALITIES, AND COUNTERFACTUALS

STUDIES IN THE LOGIC OF SCIENCE

LAWS, MODALITIES, AND COUNTERFACTUALS

HANS REICHENBACH

With a Foreword by Wesley C. Salmon

UNIVERSITY OF CALIFORNIA PRESS

Berkeley   Los Angeles   London

University of California Press
Berkeley and Los Angeles, California

University of California Press, Ltd.
London, England

ISBN: 0-520-02966-6

Library of Congress Catalog Card Number: 74-29798

The main text was originally published under the title
Nomological Statements and Admissible Operations
(Amsterdam: North-Holland Publishing Company, 1954)

Printed in the United States of America

CONTENTS

FOREWORD

Wesley C. Salmon

There is a close-knit complex of philosophical problems which has been with us since antiquity. These problems involve such concepts as potentiality and disposition; necessity, actuality, and possibility; and even material and subjunctive implication. They are philosophically ubiquitous, cropping up in a range of fields broad enough to include metaphysics, epistemology, philosophy of science, logic, philosophy of language, and ethics. They seem, moreover, to be strangely recalcitrant. It is to this set of perennial philosophical problems that Hans Reichenbach's monograph—originally published in 1954 under the title *Nomological Statements and Admissible Operations*, but here retitled *Laws, Modalities, and Counterfactuals*—is addressed. The new title will, it is hoped, provide the philosophical community with a clearer idea of the subject matter of the book.

Republication of this work, which has been out of print for many years, requires a few words of explanation. First, these problems are still with us. They have not gone away in the last twenty years. Philosophers are actively working and publishing on these topics, and no resolutions that are widely accepted as adequate are anywhere in sight.

Second, Reichenbach's monograph attracted little attention when it was first published, and it is almost completely ignored today. This lack of attention is not due to any demonstrated inadequacy in his results. Only a few philosophers seem to have been aware of the existence of this monograph, or what it is about, and those who were cognizant of it may have been repelled by its admitted complexity. Its republication is designed to bring it to the attention of philosophers who are concerned with this set of problems.

Third, Reichenbach's treatment of these problems does, I firmly believe, merit careful attention. While I do not intend to argue that he has found definitive solutions to all these problems, I do wish to urge consideration of the major concepts he develops in the course of his analysis. Even if his answers are not fully adequate, the central concepts will be enlightening to those who are working in this area. Although they embody seminal ideas, these concepts have not been generally assimilated by contemporary philosophers.

Fourth, Reichenbach's approach has philosophical virtues to recommend it. He offers a systematic account of laws, modalities, and counterfactuals which is thoroughly consonant with his empiricism. He eschews appeal to such devices as mysterious "connections" of the sort criticized by Hume, or to realms of reality reminiscent of Meinong's jungle. According to Occam's razor, postulation of such entities is to be avoided if possible. It is important to ascertain whether a satisfactory resolution of these problems can be achieved without them.

Finally, Reichenbach did not seek to evade these problems. He clearly recognized their central role in philosophy of science, as well as other areas. He spared no effort in attempting to provide answers that are adequate to the problems, and which do not violate the spirit of empiricism that characterized all his philosophical enterprises.

This Foreword, which will be devoted to elucidation and justification of the foregoing claims, will be divided into three main parts. In Part I, I shall make some general remarks about the problems, about their interrelations, and about the ways in which modern discussions have developed. This part will make it evident that Reichenbach's book is highly relevant to current philosophical concerns. In Part II, I shall discuss some basic aspects of Reichenbach's earlier attempt, in *Elements of Symbolic Logic*, to deal with the same set of problems. Although the present book is logically self-contained, the earlier treatment has, I believe, considerable heuristic value for anyone attempting to understand his subsequent, more technical, treatment. In Part III, I shall offer some hints that are intended to facilitate the understanding of *Laws, Modalities, and Counterfactuals*. Reichenbach does not give us easy answers to these problems, but he has provided a sustained and penetrating attack upon them. His work deserves serious study.

I

The most distinctive feature of twentieth-century philosophy is, perhaps, the development and widespread use of formal logic. Leibniz had envisioned the day when philosophical problems would be definitively settled by such methods, but it was not until Whitehead and Russell had produced *Principia Mathematica* that tools which might be adequate to the tasks became widely known. With the application of these resources to a variety of philosophical problems, some philosophers seemed to believe that the dream of Leibniz had come true. Logical positivists and logical empiricists, for example, sought to emphasize their reliance upon logistic techniques in the very names with which they baptized their movements.

Looking back at the results, one can hardly doubt the impact of formal logic in twentieth-century philosophy, even if the Leibnizian millennium has not as yet been realized. In the foundations of mathematics, Russell's work on paradoxes, Gödel's work on consistency and completeness, and Cohen's work on the continuum hypothesis are obvious landmarks. In semantics, Tarski's work on truth and Robinson's work on model theory stand out conspicuously. Carnap's monumental studies in inductive logic and confirmation theory rest solidly upon the foundation of formal logic. The influential studies of scientific explanation by Braithwaite, Hempel, and others stand upon the same foundations. The list is easily extended. I am not trying to give an exhaustive catalog of applications of modern logic, but only to provide a brief reminder to those of us who might now take these achievements for granted, forgetting the vast changes wrought in philosophy since the beginning of this century.

Yet, strangely enough, the problems mentioned in the opening paragraph have appeared to be amazingly refractory against the best efforts of contemporary philosophers using a variety of logical techniques. This phenomenon is all the more surprising, because the problems of modalities, lawlike generalizations, counterfactual conditionals, and dispositional predicates would seem at first blush to be precisely the sort that ought to be most amenable to formal logical analysis. The current philosophical literature, nevertheless, gives ample testimony to the absence of generally accepted solutions.

As one of the outstanding leaders of logical empiricism, Reichenbach was squarely within the tradition that places great emphasis upon logistic methods. He often reiterated his confidence in the power of formal logic to resolve philosophical problems. In his work on probability and induction, on quantum mechanics, on space and time, and on the analysis of conversational language, he attempted to exemplify the applicability of these methods. The present book constitutes his final effort to make formal methods yield answers to the puzzles associated with laws, modalities, and counterfactuals. Let us take a look at some of the background of these problems.

1. MODALITIES. The rigorous formal treatment of this ancient topic began, shortly after the publication of *Principia Mathematica*, with the work of C.I. Lewis on strict implication. C.I. Lewis developed several systems of modal logic, and other logicians have subsequently created a multitude of others. Such modal logics were formal systems containing a primitive symbol (for necessity or possibility) over and above the primitive symbols of some standard logical system. In the absence of one or more clear interpretations of the modal primitive, there was considerable room for skepticism regarding the philosophical value and import of modal logics.

Beginning about 1959, Saul Kripke and others developed rigorous semantics for modal logics. It is essential to recognize, however, that the interpretations thereby provided are abstract—that is, the entities invoked in these interpretations are mathematical constructions of one sort or another. Although the informal chat about such interpretations has involved much talk of such things as "possible worlds," the entities are, strictly speaking, entirely set-theoretical in character. A strong analogy can be drawn to analytic geometry—that is, the interpretation of the primitive terms of Euclidean geometry in terms of such extrageometrical *mathematical* entities as algebraic equations and triples of numbers. Important as the existence of such abstract interpretations is, they do not provide any enlightenment whatever to the philosopher who has questions about the structure of *physical* space. Likewise, valuable as it is to have abstract interpretations by means of which to prove completeness or consistency of modal systems, the formal systems with their abstract interpretations do not tell us anything about what is necessary or possible in the real world.[1]

In his recent book, *Counterfactuals*, David Lewis has taken the bull by the horns and asserted the reality of possible worlds. Among the real worlds one is considered actual because we happen to be living in it, but the others are no less real because of being merely possible and not actual. Denying that possible worlds are somehow to be identified with either linguistic or mathematical structures, he writes:

> When I profess realism about possible worlds, I mean to be taken literally. Possible worlds are what they are, and not some other thing. If asked what sort of thing they are, I cannot give the kind of reply my questioner probably expects: that is, a proposal to reduce possible worlds to something else.
>
> I can only ask him to admit that he knows what sort of thing our actual world is, and then explain that other worlds are more things of *that* sort,

differing not in kind but only in what goes on at them. Our actual world is only one world among others. We call it alone actual not because it differs in kind from all the rest but because it is the world we inhabit.[2]

Such shocking metaphysical proliferation requires some attempt at justification. David Lewis continues,

> So it is throughout metaphysics; and so it is with my doctrine of realism about possible worlds. Among my common opinions that philosophy must respect (if it is to deserve credence) are not only my naive belief in tables and chairs, but also my naive belief that these tables and chairs might have been otherwise arranged. Realism about possible worlds is an attempt, the only successful attempt I know of, to systematize these preexisting modal opinions.[3]

We must agree, of course, that it is sensible (and probably true) to say that tables and chairs might have been differently arranged. To those who have appreciated Russell's beautiful theory of definite descriptions as a way to make sense of statements about golden mountains, without becoming enmeshed in Meinong's jungle, David Lewis's views on the reality of possible worlds will appear to be a giant step backward. Reichenbach offered a well-developed theory of logical and physical modalities which does not indulge in such ontological excesses, but it is not cited in David Lewis's book.

The laws of nature, it might be said, delineate the realm of physical possibility; indeed, laws are often expressed quite explicitly in this form. A basic principle of relativity theory states that it is impossible to propagate any signal with a velocity greater than that of light. The first and second laws of thermodynamics, respectively, are often expressed by asserting the impossibility of perpetual motion machines of the first and second kinds. Conservation laws assert the impossibility of creating or destroying an entity or quantity of some sort. It would, of course, be foolhardy to expect modal logic (or any other kind of logic) to determine which statements express laws of nature and which statements do not.[4] But there is a more modest task—the problem of delineating the characteristics of "law-like statements," that is, the problem of specifying the characteristics a statement must have *over and above truth* if it is to express a law of nature.

If we ask whether the study of modal logic has been of any significant help in clarifying the nature of physical necessity, I think the answer must be negative. Little of the work done in modal logic has been primarily motivated by a concern with the analysis of physics (or any other empirical science).[5] The situation is just the reverse. If we had a clear grasp of the concept of physical necessity, we might be able to find a modal logic that would embody its structure. In the absence of such a prior understanding, it is unlikely that modal logic by itself will provide any insight into the nature of physical necessity.[6] Reichenbach's analysis of synthetic nomological statements—law statements—was designed to furnish clear concepts of physical modalities.

The investigations of C.I. Lewis were primarily directed, not at physical modality but rather to logical modalities. There has been considerable subsequent discussion of whether such modal systems as he constructed can capture the concept of *entailment*. Some philosophers, noting that C.I. Lewis's systems give rise to "paradoxes of strict implication," have sought what they consider a more adequate formalization of the entailment relation. The *magnum opus* on this topic has just been published.[7] In his analysis of *analytic* nomological statements (of the narrower kind), Reichenbach was attacking precisely the same sort of problem.

Philosophers have, of course, looked for other kinds of interpretations of modal logics. Some have found modal systems useful in their attempts to construct "deontic logic."[8] Others have used modal systems in an effort to characterize the nature of time; these are the "tense logics."[9] There may be many other applications of the formal structures that have been constructed under the general heading of "modal logics."[10] Interesting as they are in their own right, they do not bear upon the problems of physical modalities and laws of nature, or upon logical modalities and entailment.

2. LAWS. Concern with the nature of laws stems from a variety of sources. We have just seen that it is intimately connected with the problem of physical modalities. Another source is the extensive work—done over the past three decades—on scientific explanation. In 1948, C.G. Hempel and Paul Oppenheim published their classic article, "Studies in the Logic of Explanation," in which they formulated a basic schema of scientific explanation which has come to be known as the "deductive-nomological model."[11] One of the main requirements imposed upon such explanations is that the explanans must include at least one law-statement in an essential way. This is one among several models—elaborated by Hempel and others—which, because they require an appeal to laws of nature, are called "covering law models" of scientific explanation. The problem of providing an accurate and precise characterization of the concept of a law has been a recurrent problem in this approach to scientific explanation.[12]

Nelson Goodman's influential book, *Fact, Fiction, and Forecast*, has posed
the problem of laws in a somewhat different way.[13] By introducing certain pecu-
liar predicates he shows that some generalizations can apparently be supported
inductively by their instances, while others cannot. Goodman defines the expression, "*x* is grue at time *t*" to mean "*x* is green and $t \leq$ A.D. 2000 or *x* is
blue and $t >$ A.D. 2000." The expression "*x* is bleen at *t*" is defined in the
same manner with "blue" and "green" interchanged in the foregoing definition. Goodman then presents the "new riddle of induction" as the problem of
showing why observed instances can confirm the generalization, "All emeralds
are green," while precisely the same instances cannot confirm the generalization, "All emeralds are grue."[14] Those who would seek to resolve the problem
by admitting only "purely qualitative" predicates like "green" and "blue" into
the basic scientific vocabulary—refusing to grant inductive confirmation to
generalizations containing "positional" predicates that, like "grue" and
"bleen," involve an explicit reference to a particular time *t*—should consider
carefully Goodman's potent argument to the effect that "green" and "blue"
are the positional predicates in a language in which "grue" and "bleen" are
taken as primitive.[15] In order to answer this argument, it would seem necessary
to show that the *properties* (as opposed to predicates) *grue* and *bleen* are actually *time dependent* in a way that is relevant to the possibility of inductively confirming generalizations making reference to them.[16]
    If generalizations containing Goodmanesque predicates are suspect from the
standpoint of confirmability, they are at least equally dubious candidates for
the status of explanatory law.[17] One might wonder whether they are unconfirmable because they are nonlawlike, or whether they are nonlawlike because they
are unconfirmable. Reichenbach, as we shall see, takes the latter alternative,
making inductive verifiability *the* primary hallmark of law-statements. Given
an adequate analysis of the predicates "grue" and "bleen," Reichenbach's
requirement of universality will dispatch such statements as "All emeralds are
grue."
    In a popular introduction to philosophy of science, Hempel cites the generali-
zation, "All bodies consisting of pure gold have a mass of less than 100,000
kilograms," as presumably true, but nonlawful.[18] It would be agreed, in contrast, that the generalization, "No signal travels faster than light," is a lawful
statement. The problem is to specify the characteristics upon which this distinction rests. Reichenbach considers a similar pair of examples; I shall discuss
them in some detail below.

One immediate temptation might be to say that, although perhaps no golden object of 100,000 kilograms has ever existed, it is possible in principle to fabricate one. It is, conversely, impossible in principle to make a signal go faster than light. This answer, while true, is of no help, for it depends upon the physical modalities. As we saw in the preceding section, physical possibility and impossibility are determined by the laws of nature. The present answer thus takes us around a very neat little circle.

3. COUNTERFACTUALS. The material conditional was explicitly defined in antiquity; Sextus Empiricus presents the truth table definition, though not in a tabular form. One wonders whether ancient logicians might have drawn truth tables in the sand—after the fashion of geometers and their diagrams—in order to present the definition more concisely. Evidently there was considerable controversy among ancient philosophers concerning the nature of the conditional. Callimachus is quoted as saying, "Even the crows on rooftops are cawing over the question as to which conditionals are true."[19] The ancient logicians were fully aware of the "paradoxes of material implication."

As the beginning logic student learns while being introduced to truth tables, a material conditional with a false antecedent or with a true consequent is ipso facto true, regardless of any relation of meaning between the antecedent and consequent. The perceptive student also quickly realizes that it is very difficult to find examples of material conditionals in everyday life. "If Smith wins the election, then I'll be a monkey's uncle," which is merely a rhetorical way of expressing the speaker's confidence in the falsity of the antecedent, is about the best we can do. The vast majority of conditional statements are of the sort, "If the fuse blows, the lights will go out," or "If the fuse *were to* blow, the lights *would* go out." Because of the grammatical form of the latter sentence, the designation, "problem of subjunctive conditionals," is sometimes preferred. As long as the fuse does not blow, the conditional is counterfactual. If it were treated as a material conditional, it would be true simply because of its false antecedent. The difficulty is that the statement, "If the fuse flows, the lights will not go out," is also true for precisely the same reason. The patent unacceptability of this result shows that counterfactual conditionals have an import quite different from that of the material conditional. The problem, therefore, is to provide some adequate analysis of counterfactuals in particular, and more generally, of subjunctive conditionals.

Much of the contemporary discussion of counterfactual conditionals stems from two classic papers, one by Roderick M. Chisholm and the other by Nelson

Goodman, published in 1946 and 1947, respectively.[20] These two essays state
the basic problem in clear and engaging terms, showing that all sorts of rather
obvious moves toward resolution will not work. Chisholm's article convincingly
demonstrates the degree to which this problem reaches into a wide variety of
philosophical contexts, while Goodman's article exhibits the intimate relations
of this problem with that of laws, modalities, and dispositional properties.
Goodman treats these as problems within philosophy of science and remarks,
"...if we set aside all the problems of dispositions, possibility, scientific law,
confirmation, and the like, we virtually abandon philosophy of science."[21]
Goodman's essay was reprinted in his 1955 book, *Fact, Fiction, and Forecast*;
in the Introduction he says, "The scores of articles that have been published
since then have made so little progress toward settling the matter that current
opinion varies all the way from the view that the problem is no problem at all to
the view that it is insoluble." That statement stands unchanged in the revised
edition issued in 1965.[22] Philosophers are still working actively on the problem
of counterfactuals; as we have seen above, one of them, David Lewis, has
adopted heroic measures to resolve it.[23]

It has often been noted that acceptable counterfactual conditionals can be
"supported" by laws of nature. By examining the circuitry of the house, and by
applying laws of electricity, we can confidently predict that the lights will go off
and will not remain on if a fuse blows. As we have already noted, however, it is
no easy task to state the criteria a generalization must fulfill in order to qualify
as a law. Goodman offers as an example of a (presumed true) nonlawlike generalization the statement, "All of the coins in my pocket are silver," pointing
out that it does not support the unacceptable counterfactual, "If this penny
were in my pocket it would be made of silver." As a contrasting example of a
lawlike generalization—which now brings a twinge of nostalgia—he offers the
statement, "All dimes are silver," which presumably does support the counterfactual conditional, "If this coin (which happens to be a penny) were a dime, it
would be made of silver." The difficulty is that a law-like generalization is just
the sort of generalization that could support counterfactuals, while a nonlawlike generalization cannot. Again, we have gone in a circle. A reasonable
counterfactual is one that is supported by a law, while a generalization is a law
provided it can lend support to counterfactual assertions.

4. DISPOSITIONS. One of the most pervasive philosophical influences in
modern science—due more to scientists than to philosophers—is the viewpoint
known as operationism. The operationist thesis is, briefly, that a scientific con-

cept cannot be meaningful unless its applicability is associated with some sort of physical operation. A metal rod is one meter long if its ends coincide with the ends of a suitably situated meter stick. A piece of iron is magnetic if it attracts nearby iron filings. Such "operational definitions" clearly have a conditional form. To say that the piece of iron is magnetic *means* iron filings will be attracted *if* they are in the neighborhood. If we want to say, as most scientists presumably would, that the rod is one meter long whether it is actually being measured at the moment or not, and that the piece of iron is magnetic whether there happen to be any iron filings in the vicinity at the moment or not, then obviously these operational definitions embody counterfactual conditionals. Operationists, by and large, have not concerned themselves with the analysis of counterfactual conditionals, apparently believing that our common sense understanding of this type of statement is adequate for all practical purposes. Yet, if one were to try to analyze these definitions in terms of material conditionals, absurd results would ensue. A piece of glass which had never been placed near any iron filings would qualify as magnetic. Operationists, who pride themselves on their precision, would presumably applaud efforts to find a clear analysis of such conditionals.

The classic attempt to provide a precise logical analysis of operational definitions, and definitions of dispositional predicates in general, is Carnap's "Testability and Meaning."[24] In order to avoid problems surrounding the material conditional, Carnap constructs so-called *reduction sentences* which are to serve as partial definitions of scientific terms. A typical reduction sentence might read,

If x has iron filings in its vicinity, then x is magnetic if and only
   if the iron filings are attracted to x.

In this statement, the conditional and the biconditional are to be construed as material. The import of the partial definition is that x is judged magnetic or nonmagnetic only if iron filings are nearby; if there are no iron filings in the vicinity the reduction sentence remains true, but no conclusion whatever can be drawn about the magnetic character of x. Another reduction sentence could be introduced to provide a further definition of the term "magnetic."

If x is moved through a coil of conducting wire, then
   x is magnetic if and only if a current flows in the coil.

By furnishing additional reduction sentences, we can more fully specify the meaning of a dispositional concept.

It is now generally recognized, I believe, that Carnap's reduction sentences, ingenious as they are, do not really handle the problem of dispositional concepts, for the dispositional predicate can only be meaningfully applied if one or another of the test conditions—for example, having iron filings in the vicinity or being moved through a conducting coil—is satisfied. The problem of dispositional terms is precisely that of specifying conditions for their applicability when *no* test conditions happen to obtain.[25] It appears that a subjunctive conditional is what we need for this purpose. Thus, the problem of dispositional concepts falls neatly into place along with the problems of counterfactuals, laws, and modalities.

It is worth noting that an increasing number of philosophers have recently been adopting the "propensity interpretation" of probability. According to this interpretation, a probability is a *dispositional property* of a "chance set-up." Unlike such traditional dispositions as inflammability or solubility, propensities are statistical dispositions to manifest a certain outcome, not in all cases in which the conditions are satisfied, but in a certain percentage of such cases. Like the standard dispositions, the statistical dispositions also have a counterfactual import. For example, a penny that was placed on a railroad track and flattened by a passing train before it was ever flipped could still have been said to have had a propensity of one-half for showing heads *if it had been flipped in the prescribed manner*. This concept of probability has been the subject of a large and growing literature within the last few years, and it constitutes still another locus of the problems of dispositions and counterfactuals.

The cluster of problems concerning modalities, laws, counterfactuals, and dispositions remains a matter of serious concern to philosophers interested in modal logic, entailment, scientific explanation, inductive logic ("projectability"), probability, operational definitions, counterfactual conditionals, determinism and free will ("avoidability"), and a host of other major issues. Let us now take a look at Reichenbach's earlier attempt to provide a systematic resolution.

II

In 1947, Hans Reichenbach published *Elements of Symbolic Logic.*[26] Its final chapter is devoted to the problems of laws, modalities, and counterfactuals.

One of Reichenbach's major concerns in this book was to show how symbolic logic could be used for the analysis of conversational language. When he first introduces the truth table definitions of the truth-functional operations, he is careful to emphasize the profound differences between their strictly truth-functional interpretation and the interpretations of such connectives when they occur in conversational language—including, it should be emphasized, the ordinary language of science. He attempts to explain this difference in terms of two distinct ways of reading truth tables.[27] One way of reading yields what he calls "adjunctive operations," the other what he calls "connective operations." The material implication is adjunctive; the subjunctive implication is a connective operation.

This distinction between adjunctive and connective interpretations obviously applies to equivalences just as it does to implications—the material equivalence is simply a conjunction of two material implications. Reichenbach realized that a similar distinction applies to two ways of interpreting a disjunction. When a gun-brandishing bandit says, "If you do not give me your money, I'll blow your head off," his statement would normally be understood in the subjunctive or connective sense. If, after handing over your money, you notice that the gun he holds is a toy, you might chide him for issuing a false threat. If he has studied symbolic logic he could reply that his implication was true—since you handed over your money, it has a false antecedent. The same threat could obviously have been couched in the form of a disjunction: "You will give me your money or I will blow your head off." The ensuing dialogue can easily be constructed. Recognizing clearly that the problem at hand was more general than the interpretation of conditional statements, Reichenbach posed it in terms of "connective operations" in general.

I have never found Reichenbach's explanations of the relations between adjunctive and connective operations in terms of two ways of reading the truth tables particularly helpful. The main reason is that this explanation relies heavily upon the use of "connective operations" in the metalanguage—a point that Reichenbach recognized explicitly and, with characteristic philosophic candor, commented upon.[28] These preliminary discussions of the truth tables are not question begging; they are merely informal attempts at clarification. The actual analysis of the connective operations is reserved for the last chapter, where it is treated in the context of logical and physical laws, and logical and physical modalities. Although Reichenbach's subsequent treatment of these problems in the book here reprinted is logically self-contained, I believe an understanding of some of the material from *Elements of Symbolic Logic* may be heuristically valuable. Most of the main thrust of his later treatment is contained in this earlier discussion. *Laws, Modalities, and Counterfactuals* embodies important revisions and refinements, but the earlier account provides an excellent point of departure.

Reichenbach's first major task is to define the class of *original nomological statements*. This class is intended to contain both the fundamental laws of logic and the fundamental laws of nature. The qualifying term "fundamental" is important, for he maintains that there are *derivative nomological statements*; these include both laws of logic and laws of nature which do not qualify as fundamental. Original nomological statements, as defined in *Elements of Symbolic Logic*, must fulfill four requirements.[29] In this earlier work, unlike the present book, Reichenbach was not very careful to distinguish criteria that depend upon the form in which a statement is given from those that depend solely upon its content. Since I am not offering a critique of the earlier treatment, I shall attempt to capture his intent, even if his explicit statement sometimes falls a bit short. The criteria are:

1. Original nomological statements must be *all-statements*. An all-statement is simply a statement that begins with an all-operator which has the entire statement as its scope. (Reichenbach used the term "all-operator" for what is now usually called a "universal quantifier"; I shall follow his usage.) Clearly, this requirement relates partly to the form of the statement. It would seem to capture Reichenbach's intent, however, to stipulate that the statement first be transformed into a prenex form—an equivalent statement with operators initially placed and having the entire formula as scope—and then to apply the test to see whether it qualifies as an all-statement. If it does, then the given statement, even if it is not originally formulated with an initial all-operator whose scope is the whole statement, would qualify as an all-statement. Being equivalent to a statement that has the requisite form, the given statement would certainly possess the type of generality we want to demand of fundamental laws.

2. Original nomological statements must be *universal*. A statement is defined as universal if it contains no individual-signs—for example, proper names, definite descriptions, designators of particular space-time locations, and so forth. Again, the criterion makes reference to the form of the statement, for a statement that contains an individual-sign may be transformed into an equivalent statement that does not, and vice-versa. In *Laws, Modalities, and Counterfactuals*, Reichenbach is very careful to spell out the requirement in detail, but

in the earlier treatment he was not as precise. The intent, nevertheless, is straightforward; a fundamental law must not make essential reference to any individual entity. It is worth noting that, because of this criterion, neither Galileo's law of falling bodies (which makes essential reference to the Earth) nor Kepler's law of planetary motion (which make essential reference to our Solar System) would qualify as fundamental laws. They would, however, qualify as derivative nomological statements.[30]

3. Original nomological statements must be *fully exhaustive*. Requirements of the first two types are familiar from practically every discussion of the nature of laws. This third requirement is not generally mentioned; it demands fuller explanation. If a given statement is transformed into a prenex form, with all operators standing in front and having scopes that extend to the end of the formula, then that portion of the formula which does not contain the operators—what Reichenbach calls the "operand"—can be expanded in either of two ways. (i) *Expansion in major terms*. The operand has a truth-functional structure, and as such, it has a major operation. If, for example, the operand has the form $A \supset B$, regardless of the internal structures of the components A and B, then it can be expanded into a formula with the form $A \cdot B \lor \bar{A} \cdot B \lor \bar{A} \cdot \bar{B}$.[31] It is a disjunctive normal form where A and B are treated as unanalyzed units; A and B are the *terms* of the major operation. Reichenbach now defines a *residual statement in major terms* as a statement that results by dropping one or more of the disjuncts of the expanded operand (along with a suitable number of disjunction symbols). The residual statement thus consists of the set of prefixed quantifiers followed by an operand expanded in major terms, less one or more of the disjuncts of the expanded operand.

A true statement is said to be *exhaustive in major terms* if none of its residual statements in major terms is true. The concept of exhaustiveness is not defined for false statements. As the fourth requirement will stipulate, original nomological statements must be true, so we have no need to apply the concept of exhaustiveness to false statements.

The requirement of exhaustiveness in major terms disqualifies universal statements with empty antecedents from the class of original nomological statements. Consider, for example, the statement, "All unicorns are four-legged." Expanded in major terms, it becomes

$$(x)[u(x) \cdot f(x) \lor \overline{u(x)} \cdot f(x) \lor \overline{u(x)} \cdot \overline{f(x)}].$$

Since there are no unicorns, the following residual statement is true:

$$(x)[\overline{u(x)} . f(x) \vee \overline{u(x)} . \overline{f(x)}].$$

Somewhat surprisingly, perhaps, it also excludes from the class of original nomological statements such statements as "All animals that (naturally) have hearts also (naturally) have kidneys," which, expanded in major terms, becomes,

$$(x)[h(x) . k(x) \vee \overline{h(x)} . k(x) \vee \overline{h(x)} . \overline{k(x)}].$$

Since (I believe) only animals with hearts have kidneys, the following residual is true:

$$(x)[h(x) . k(x) \vee \overline{h(x)} . \overline{k(x)}].$$

This statement does, however, qualify as derivative nomological (in the narrower as well as the wider sense). Reichenbach offers the following justification for invoking the exhaustiveness requirement: "If an all-statement is not exhaustive in its major terms, its major operation is used out of place, so to speak; the operation then suggests connections which do not exist."[32]

(ii) *Expansion in elementary terms.* If a quantified statement, in prenex form, has operand with more than a single truth-functional operation, that operand can be expanded into its full disjunctive normal form. Consider, for example, an operand of the form $A \supset (B \supset C)$, where A, B, and C have no internal truth-functional structure. Its disjunctive normal form would be

$$A.B.C \vee A.\overline{B}.C \vee A.\overline{B}.\overline{C} \vee \overline{A}.B.C \vee \overline{A}.B.\overline{C} \vee \overline{A}.\overline{B}.C \vee \overline{A}.\overline{B}.\overline{C}$$

A residual statement in elementary terms is defined in the same fashion as a residual statement in major terms; it is the statement that results from deleting one or more of the disjuncts of the expansion in elementary terms. A true statement is *exhaustive in elementary terms* if none of its residual statements in elementary terms is true. Again, there is no need to define this concept with respect to false all-statements.

Finally, a statement is *fully exhaustive* if it is exhaustive both in major terms and in elementary terms. This is the property original nomological statements must possess, according to requirement 3. This requirement is a stringent prohibition against many types of vacuousness in statements that are to qualify as original nomological. It is important to note that the residual is stronger, not weaker than the given statement. Statements that fail the test of exhaustiveness do so because they say too little, not too much.

4. Original nomological statements must be *demonstrable as true*. This requirement is, in a sense, the crucial one, and it introduces a number of serious problems. As a first step, it is essential to distinguish between *analytic* and *synthetic* original nomological statements. Those of the analytic variety are the basic laws of logic, and their truth is demonstrated by showing them to be theorems of the logical system to which they belong.[33] Nothing more need be said about them at this juncture.

Synthetic original nomological statements are more problematic. Such statements must be demonstrated inductively, or, in the terms used in the present book, verified inductively. Such demonstration or verification cannot be conclusive in the way that deductive demonstration is; it must consist in strong inductive confirmation or great weight of inductive evidence. Reichenbach says such statements are "verified as *practically true* at some time during the past, present, or future history of mankind."[34] This strikes me as a rather awkward way of saying that synthetic original nomological statements must be true, and that evidence exists which would provide warrant for asserting them, not with absolute certainty, but with a high degree of inductive reliability. Reichenbach carefully avoids saying that it must be *possible* to obtain inductive evidence, for he does not want to risk the circularity of using the concept of possibility which is yet to be explicated in his ensuing theory of physical modalities.

The fundamental aim of Reichenbach's whole theory of synthetic original nomological statements is to insure that "the assertion of such statements is necessarily left to the methods of induction."[35] The foregoing three requirements imposed upon synthetic original nomological statements are designed to guarantee that they cannot be verified by any other methods. (1) "Some swans are black," for example, violates the requirement of being an all-statement. It can be verified by direct observation, without involving any process of inductive generalization. (2) "All coins in my pocket at present are silver" violates the requirement of universality. It can be verified by complete enumeration, without any use of inductive generalization. (3) "All unicorns are four-legged" violates the requirement of exhaustiveness. This violation indicates that the statement in question does not have the full generality that the inductive evidence warrants. Consider its contrapositive, "All non-four-legged animals are non-unicorns." The available inductive evidence obviously justifies a stronger generalization, namely, "All animals are non-unicorns." Since the latter statement *does* fulfill all requirements, *it* should be taken as original nomological. The former statement is not verified by direct inductive generalization; it is asserted on the basis of our knowledge of the emptiness of its antecedent, which follows from the latter generalization.

Requirement (4), demonstrability as true, is designed to insure that statements, whose truth cannot be certified by other means, can be established (to some suitable degree) by inductive methods. Reichenbach offers a concrete example to illustrate this condition:

> Thus the statement, 'all gold cubes are smaller than one cubic mile' may be true; but since we cannot prove it to be true it is no nomological statement. We thus exclude statements that are true by chance. Such exclusion is in accordance with our maxim of reducing the definition. . . to the methods of inductive evidence.[36]

This attempt to explain the force of the requirement of demonstrability as true is singularly unilluminating. It appears that Reichenbach is saying that the statement about gold cubes is not a nomological statement because it is "true by chance," which seems to mean that, if true, it is not lawful—that is, it is not nomological. All this passage seems to say is that "All gold cubes are smaller than one cubic mile" is not nomological because it is not nomological. The discussion in *Elements of Symbolic Logic* offers no further help in understanding this requirement. Reichenbach seems to be allowing his account of lawfulness to rest upon our unanalyzed ability to distinguish those generalizations that can be supported by inductive evidence from those that cannot. As we saw above, in the discussion of Goodman's "grue-bleen paradox," one important way of formulating the fundamental problem of laws, counterfactuals, and dispositions is in terms of the problem of analyzing the difference between those generalizations that can be supported by inductive evidence and those that cannot. Reichenbach's treatment in *Elements of Symbolic Logic* seems to beg this very question.

Reichenbach published his logic book in 1947, the year immediately following Goodman's first publication of this famous problem. Reichenbach was evidently unaware of it at the time he wrote the foregoing passage on the statement about gold cubes. By 1949, when he published *The Theory of Probability* (the English translation and revised edition of *Wahrscheinlichkeitslehre*), he was aware of Goodman's puzzle, and he offered what he considered an appropriate resolution of it.[37] It is my impression that he did not take Goodman's problem very seriously, and I am not satisfied that his solution is adequate. This was, of course, earlier than the posthumous publication of *Nomological Statements and Admissible Operations* (1954).

It is my view, as mentioned above, that Reichenbach's theory of nomological statements should handle Goodman's example, "All emeralds are grue," by saying that it violates his condition of universality on account of the positional character of the predicate "grue." This answer would certainly seem appropriate if we have an adequate way of establishing the fundamental positionality of "grue" and "bleen" which does not fall victim to Goodman's symmetry argument. I believe I have furnished the essentials of such an analysis.[38] Goodman's argument, and the widespread lack of consensus on its appropriate resolution should, nevertheless, make us strongly suspicious of any claim that there is an easy or obvious distinction between generalizations that can be supported by inductive evidence and generalizations that cannot.

In *Laws, Modalities, and Counterfactuals*, Reichenbach offers some further illumination. (1) He points out the obvious fact that this book is not intended to provide an analysis of inductive evidence. For answers to questions about the nature of inductive evidence we must consult his other writings on the subject, especially *The Theory of Probability*. (2) He offers some further remarks about the gold cube example:

> When we reject a statement of this kind as not expressing a law of nature, we mean to say that observable facts do not require any such statement for their interpretation and thus do not confer any truth, or any degree of probability, on it. If they did, if we had good inductive evidence for the statement, we would be willing to accept it. For instance, the statement, 'all signals are slower than or equally fast as light signals', is accepted as a law of nature because observable facts confer a high probability upon it. It is the inductive verification, not mere truth, which makes an all-statement a law of nature. In fact, if we could prove that gold cubes of giant size would condense under gravitational pressure into a sun-like gas ball whose atoms were all disintegrated, we would be willing also to accept the statement about gold cubes among the laws of nature.[39]

This passage is, if not explicitly enlightening, at least suggestive. For one thing, it serves to remind us that the statement, "No signal travels faster than light," has been tested experimentally to some extent. The attempt to accelerate electrons to superlight velocities has resulted in velocities that asymptotically approach that of light, but never reach or exceed it. Moreover, all the experimental evidence—of which an enormous amount exists—supporting the special theory of relativity at least indirectly supports the assertion that no signals exceed the speed of light. The statement about gold cubes, in contrast, has never—to the best of our knowledge—been subjected to experimental test. This certainly represents a crucial difference between the two generalizations. If asked why the statement about gold cubes has never been tested, we could answer that there is no theoretical interest in performing what would inevitably be an extraordinarily expensive experiment. This calls attention to another—closely related—difference. Even if we were to verify the statement about gold cubes, it would not have any explanatory import that we can foresee.

(3) In the Appendix of *Laws, Modalities, and Counterfactuals*, Reichenbach does deal with certain important features of the inductive verification of all-statements. The most significant point is the vast difference between the establishing of a probability—even a probability approximately equal to one—by induction by enumeration, on the one hand, and the inductive verification of an original nomological statement, on the other. This distinction is signaled unmistakably by the fact that limiting frequencies (probabilities) can be posited in *primitive knowledge*, while lawful generalizations can only be established in *advanced knowledge*. *There are no synthetic nomological statements in primitive knowledge.*

If one approaches both statements, "All gold cubes are smaller than one cubic mile" and "All signals have velocities less than or equal to that of light," from the standpoint of simple enumeration in primitive knowledge, it is hard to discern any difference. We can equally assert that all observed gold cubes fall below the size mentioned and that all observed signals have velocities that fall below the mentioned limit. Thus we might posit that the probability of a gold cube being less than one cubic mile in size is one, and the probability that a signal will have a velocity not exceeding that of light is also one. It is, of course, ludicrous—given the considerable theoretical content of both of these statements—to suppose that either could be treated in primitive knowledge. But let us keep up the fiction for a moment in order to see what more is needed.

Reichenbach considers the question of what kind of evidence is required to establish a generalization of the form "All A's are B." There are three main conditions to be satisfied. First, we must have evidence that $P(A,B)$—the probability that an A is a B—is high. That is the kind of evidence we have already mentioned, and we are assuming that it exists for both of the generalizations we are discussing. Second, we must consider evidence for the contrapositive "All non-B's are non-A." This evidence must be considered independently, for we cannot infer that the probability $P(\bar{B},\bar{A})$ is high from the fact that the probability $P(A,B)$ is high. From the fact that most kind people are nonphilosophers (because most people are nonphilosophers), we obviously cannot infer that most philosophers are unkind. Since contraposition is a valid transformation when applied to universal generalizations, but not when applied to probability relations, we must first establish inductively the high probability of the contrapositive, if we want to make a transition from a statement of high probability to an all-statement.

Let us return to the examples we were considering. There is considerable inductive evidence to support the view that all things with velocities greater than light are nonsignals. This point is elaborated in some detail in Reichenbach's *Philosophy of Space and Time*.[40] Although we may have some inductive evidence for the assertion that all things larger than one cubic mile are not gold cubes, one can hardly claim that any systematic effort has ever been made to find a gold cube among the objects of that size.

The third requirement—which is probably the most important in this context —deals with partitions or restrictions of the reference class. Given an all statement, "All A's are B," we can immediately deduce the restricted statement "All A's that are C's are B." From the statement, "All men are mortal," we can obviously conclude, "All men over six feet tall are mortal." Again—as with contraposition—this relation has no analogue for high probability statements. From the fact that it is very probable that a man of forty will survive for another year we obviously cannot conclude that it is probable that a forty-year-old man with an advanced case of lung cancer will survive for another year. Again, if we want to make the transition from a high probability statement to an all-statement, we must consider independently whether we have evidence to support the claim that the high probability will be sustained under restrictions on the reference class.[41]

Let us indulge in a little science fiction. Suppose that on a planet orbiting a star in a distant galaxy there is a race of highly intelligent, technologically sophisticated beings with an intense interest in rapid communication. Can we say with confidence that all signals sent by such beings travel with velocities not exceeding that of light? I believe an affirmative answer is justified. Suppose that such beings also have intense aesthetic admiration for gold cubes—the bigger the better. Suppose, further, that the planet these beings inhabit is richly endowed with gold. Can we say with comparable confidence that all gold cubes fabricated by these beings are smaller than one cubic mile? The answer, I believe, must be negative. This third consideration at least lends a bit of plausibility to the claim that the all-statement about signals differs from the all-statement about gold cubes in specifiable ways that bear upon their nomological status.

An additional point deserves explicit mention. In his theory of probability, Reichenbach attempted to defend the claim that Bayes's theorem provides the schema for the inductive support of scientific hypotheses by observational evidence. Although his discussion of this thesis was not easy to understand, its main outline can be discerned.[42] When one considers an all-statement from the standpoint of the requirement of demonstrability as true, it is *incorrect* to approach it in terms of induction by enumeration. Rather, the statement must be taken as one that has to satisfy the three above-mentioned requirements for transition from a high-probability-statement to an all-statement, and its evidence has to be evaluated within the schema provided by Bayes's theorem. When we ask whether an all-statement is inductively verified, we must consider the degree to which it has been subjected to observational and/or experimental testing within the bayesian framework, and how strongly all the accumulated evidence supports it. This schema involves reference to prior probabilities, and to the possibility of explaining the data by means of alternative hypotheses, as well as any direct instantial confirming evidence.

The purpose of my discussion of Reichenbach's requirement of *demonstrability as true* has not been to argue that he has provided an entirely satisfactory account of the inductive support of scientific hypotheses. I have merely been trying to show that this requirement—Requirement 1.1 in *Laws, Modalities, and Counterfactuals*—is not trivially question-begging. I urge the reader to turn to the Appendix upon encountering the term, "verifiably true," in this book. It is especially important not to allow the difficulties surrounding Requirement 1.1 to constitute a major obstacle to digging into the detail of Reichenbach's deep but highly technical treatment of laws, modalities, and counterfactuals.

As we approach the treatment of original nomological statements in *Laws, Modalities, and Counterfactuals,* we shall be able to make good use of Reichenbach's explication of that concept from *Elements of Symbolic Logic:*

> *An original nomological statement is an all-statement that is demonstrably true, fully exhaustive, and universal.*[43]

It will be advisable to keep clearly in mind the fact that his main purpose in these discussions of original nomological statements is to lay down requirements that will *exclude* generalizations that can be verified in any way other than by inductive generalization—not in the crude sense of primitive induction by enumeration but in the sophisticated schema furnished by Bayes's theorem. His extensive discussions of inductive verification are given in other works— mainly *The Theory of Probability*—and they are not repeated in either of these treatments of original nomological statements.

III

Having discussed some basic aspects of Reichenbach's treatment of original nomological statements in *Elements of Symbolic Logic*, I shall now offer some remarks on the content of the present book which, it is hoped, will make the reader's job in tackling this complex body of material somewhat easier. The principal features of the earlier treatment are carried over into this later work, but the details had to be modified considerably to meet certain objections raised by critics, and other objections Reichenbach himself discovered. In this book, for example, Reichenbach takes pains to distinguish I-terms and I-requirements (terms and requirements that do not depend upon the form in which the statement is given, and which are therefore *invariant* with respect to the linguistic form) from V-terms and V-requirements (terms and requirements that do depend upon the linguistic form, and which are therefore *variant*). I commented above upon his failure to handle this distinction adequately in his earlier treatment. There are many other revisions as well; altogether they result in a great increase in the complexity of the theory.

In *Laws, Modalities, and Counterfactuals,* as in *Elements of Symbolic Logic,*

Reichenbach's initial goal is to define the class of original nomological statements. This class contains both analytic and synthetic statements, and in the ensuing development as well, Reichenbach attempts to construct a unified theory in which *logical* laws and modalities are treated along with *physical* laws and modalities. While there are parallels between the two types of laws and modalities, it seems to me that it would be heuristically advantageous to construct two distinct theories—pointing out interesting parallels where they exist—rather than combining the two into one. The desirability of this approach is indicated by the fact that certain terms are I-terms for synthetic statements but V-terms for analytic statements, as well as by the fact that some requirements apply to synthetic statements but not to analytic statements.[44] Throughout Chapter II, in which the basic definitions are given, frequent exceptions must be introduced on account of analytic statements, and in subsequent elaborations the reader is frequently distracted by further distinctions and exceptions. In the discussion that is to follow, I shall adopt the approach that separates analytic from synthetic statements.

1. *Analytic statements and operations.* Original nomological statements of the analytic type constitute basic logical laws, and they provide the source from which logical necessity originates. The definition of analytic original nomological statements in this book contains many refinements on that of *Elements of Symbolic Logic*, but no basic changes in substance. Given the definition of original nomological statements, Reichenbach then goes on to define the class of *derivative nomological statements*. This class contains all statements that can be deduced from the analytic original nomological statements. The class of derivative nomological statements *in the wider sense* contains all statements deducible in any way from the original nomological statements. Since all statements in the class of analytic original nomological statements are logically necessary, and since any statement that follows necessarily from a logically necessary statement is itself logically necessary, the class of analytic derivative nomological statements (in conjunction with the class of analytic original nomological statements) defines the concept of logical necessity. The other logical modalities can, of course, be defined in terms of logical necessity.

By imposing certain restrictions (to be discussed below) upon the class of nomological statements, Reichenbach defines the class of analytic derivative nomological statements *in the narrower sense*. These restrictions are designed to block such "unreasonable" analytic implications as

$$a \cdot \bar{a} \supset b$$

Reichenbach's aim is evidently to deal with such problems as the "paradoxes of strict implication." He is also attempting to define a set of "admissible operations" which, it seems to me, might capture some of the relations that have been of interest to logicians concerned with relevant entailment. Within the realm of analytic statements, with his analysis of original nomological statements, derivative nomological statements in the broader sense, and derivative nomological statements in the narrower sense, Reichenbach claims to have provided an adequate explication of the concepts of logical law, logical modality, and admissible logical operation.

2. *Synthetic statements and operations.* Reichenbach explicitly remarks that his main interest lies in synthetic statements; his primary motivation is to explicate the concept of a law of nature, along with the related concepts of physical modalities and reasonable synthetic operations. From this point on, I shall confine my discussion to synthetic nomological statements, and I shall omit the qualifying adjective "synthetic."

In Chapter III of *Laws, Modalities, and Counterfactuals,* Reichenbach presents his analysis of original nomological statements. This explication is preceded by twenty-six definitions, some rather abstruse, set out in Chapter II. Since the reader is apt to get bogged down in a morass of terminology before getting to the requirements that must be satisfied by a statement p, if it is to qualify as original nomological, it might be helpful if I were to attempt an overview of the theory Reichenbach is developing. I shall therefore discuss the requirements on original nomological statements, informally showing what each of them is driving at, and giving some indication of the reasons for the preceding set of definitions. The requirements are divided into two groups; there are five I-requirements (requirements that are invariant with respect to the particular linguistic formulation of a statement) and four V-requirements (requirements that do depend upon the linguistic form in which the statement is given). I shall begin with the five I-requirements.

The I-requirements in the present book strongly resemble the requirements for original nomological statements set forth in *Elements of Symbolic Logic.* There are three important differences, and I shall comment upon them in due course. According to Requirement 1.1, the statement p must be verifiably true. This requirement is the counterpart of the earlier requirement that the statement be demonstrably true; I have discussed the import of this requirement above. Reichenbach's theory of nomological statements—laws of nature—is, I believe, unintelligible if this fundamental requirement is not clearly understood. The remaining four I-requirements are designed to capture four distinct types of generality original nomological statements must possess. Three of these types of generality were mentioned in the requirements in *Elements of Symbolic Logic,* namely, the statement *p* must be universal, an all-statement, and exhaustive. Requirements 1.2, 1.3, and 1.4, respectively, state these requirements. The fourth generality condition, Requirement 1.5—that *p* must be general in self-contained factors—is new. The addition of this requirement is the first of the important differences mentioned above. In order to articulate these conditions of generality, Reichenbach introduces several distinct kinds of normal forms. The basic function of the definitions of Chapter II is to characterize these normal forms and relate them to his generality requirements. A number of these definitions clarify the meanings of concepts used without explicit definition in *Elements of Symbolic Logic.*

As we saw above, the requirement of universality—Requirement 1.2—prohibits the statement *p* from making explicit or implicit reference to individuals or restricted space-time regions. In order to carry through this requirement, Reichenbach has to introduce the notion of a *reduced statement*—roughly, one that contains no redundant parts. Chapter II contains a definition of that concept, and a procedure for carrying out a reduction. Requirements 1.2-1.5 do not require *p* to be a reduced statement, but universality does demand that *p* not be logically equivalent to any reduced statement that contains an individual-term. The basic aim is to insure that, if *p* contains an individual-term, it occurs inessentially or redundantly, and moreover, that *p* not contain any implicit reference to particular individuals or restricted space-time regions. In the new version of *Laws, Modalities, and Counterfactuals*, Requirement 1.4 (exhaustiveness) helps to carry some of this burden. But the intent of the new requirements is to formulate more precisely the condition of universality that was articulated in the earlier explication of original nomological statements.

Requirements 1.3 demands that *p* be an all-statement. This requirement reads exactly like one of the earlier requirements, but its meaning has been changed. This change is unmentioned by Reichenbach, but it seems rather significant; this is the second of three above-mentioned changes. In order to apply the requirement that *p* be an all-statement, it is necessary to transform *p* into a prenex form—that is, an equivalent formula whose operators are all initially placed with scopes extending to the end. In *Elements of Symbolic Logic, p* was an all-statement if and only if the *initial* operator in its prenex form was an all-operator.[45] In *Laws, Modalities, and Counterfactuals*, the requirement is considerably weaker; it is enough that the set of operators in the prenex form contain an all-operator.[46] Thus, for both versions of the requirement,

$$(x)(\exists y)[f(x) \supset g(y) . h(x,y)],$$

qualifies as an all-statement, while

$$(\exists y)(x)[f(x) \supset g(y) . h(x,y)]$$

would not have qualified as an all-statement under the earlier requirement, but does qualify under the present requirement. Examining the contexts, I find it hard to believe that this change was made inadvertently.[47] At the same time, it is unlike Reichenbach to make such a significant change without comment.

Regardless of Reichenbach's intent, this modification of the all-statement requirement demands serious consideration. It seems clear that certain statements with both universal and existential operators—for example, every atom contains at least one proton—qualify as laws. This is unproblematic because the universal operator precedes the existential operator. It is more difficult to decide whether a statement with an existential operator preceding all universal operators should be allowed to qualify as a fundamental law. I do not know of any general argument against admitting some such statements as laws, and several plausible examples come to mind. Perhaps such statements as "There is a field of 3°K black body radiation in which every object in the universe is immersed," "There is a quantum of action which must occur in integral amounts in every physical interaction," or "There is a universal constant of gravitation G which determines the force of attraction between any two bodies of given masses at a given distance from one another," might qualify as original nomological. It might be argued, of course, that some or all these statements should be relegated to the status of derivative nomological; at the same time, the fact that the last example is the denial of "Mach's principle" suggests that it enjoys a fundamental status. The question of whether statements that, in prenex form, have an initial existential operator should be allowed to qualify as original nomological statements is an issue to which philosophers should, I think, devote some careful deliberation.[48]

Having transformed a statement into a prenex form, we must go one step far-
ther and transform its operand into a disjunctive normal form (D-form) in
order to apply the condition of exhaustiveness—Requirement 1.4. The further
concept of a residual (discussed above) is also needed. Although the present formulation of the requirement of exhaustiveness differs in detail from the previous version, the intent is clearly the same. It will be recalled from our previous
discussion that the requirement of exhaustiveness is designed to insure that the
general statements that qualify as original nomological should be as fully general as the inductive evidence permits. This requirement is designed to rule out
certain kinds of vacuously true statements, such as those with empty antecedents, but it also blocks other types of vacuousness which are similar in principle. The requirement applies to statements whose major operations are not
implications; it also applies to statements, with both kinds of operators, which
suffer from vacuousness related to the existential operator rather than the universal operator. Reichenbach shows, for example, that statements of the form

$$(x)(\exists y)[f(x,y) \supset g(x,y)]$$

may be vacuous, but not because of an always-false antecedent.[49]

Requirement 1.5, demanding that p be *general in self-contained factors,* did
not appear in the earlier treatment of original nomological statements. This
requirement is motivated by the fact that a statement that consists, for example,
of a conjunction of an all-statement and an existential statement, can be transformed into a prenex form that fulfills the preceding three generality requirements; because of the purely existential part, such statements should not, however, be taken as original nomological. Consider, for instance, a statement of
the form

$$(x)(\exists y)\left\{ [f(x) \supset g(x)] \cdot h(y) \right\},$$

which is equivalent to

$$(x)[f(x) \supset g(x)] \cdot (\exists y)h(y).$$

"All metal objects expand when heated and whales exist" exemplifies this form.
The first conjunct may certainly qualify as an original nomological statement,

but the second conjunct cannot, for it is not an all-statement. We surely do not want to allow the conjunction of an original nomological statement with a purely existential statement to qualify as original nomological. This statement violates requirement 1.5.

In order to explain what is meant by "being general in self-contained factors," Reichenbach has to introduce still another type of normal form, the conjunctive normal form or C-form. A residual of a C-form is defined analogously to a residual of a D-form. Requirement 1.5 simply demands that the residuals of the C-forms be all-statements.

We can now give a rough summary of the I-requirements for original nomological statements:

> An original nomological statement is a true statement that is inductively verifiable and possesses the following four types of generality: (1) it is universally quantified; (2) it contains no implicit or explicit reference to particular individuals or restricted regions of space-time; (3) it is as fully general as the inductive evidence permits; and (4) it cannot be decomposed into independent conjunctive parts with any part failing to be universally quantified.

This set of conditions, which is, of course, spelled out much more fully and precisely in *Laws, Modalities, and Counterfactuals*, seems to me to deserve careful consideration as a reasonable set of qualifications for statements that purport to state fundamental laws of nature.

Reichenbach goes on, however, to impose four additional V-requirements. It would be natural to ask why he bothers with such conditions. Would it not be adequate to spell out the I-requirements (as he has done) and leave it at that, admitting that any statement, regardless of the form in which it is stated, is original nomological if it fulfills the I-requirements? This would be tantamount to saying that any statement that is logically equivalent to an original nomological statement also qualifies as original nomological. Why is he unwilling to accept this approach?

The answer lies in the fact that Reichenbach is trying to characterize not only basic law statements but also reasonable propositional operations. These operations, we recall, are needed to deal with such problems as the nature of the subjunctive conditional statement. Near the end of Chapter III, Reichenbach states his aim with regard to reasonable operations: ". . . propositional operations can be called reasonable when they stand as major operations of original nomological statements."[50] It is obvious that two logically equivalent statements can have different major operations, so having a particular major operation is not an I-property of statements. It is also apparent that, if one is free to perform any equivalence transformation, redundancies can be introduced in such a way as to render the major operation "unreasonable." Thus, a statement of the form

$$(x)[f(x) \supset g(x)]$$

is logically equivalent to one having the form

$$(x)[h(x) \lor \overline{h(x)} \supset \overline{f(x)} \lor g(x)];$$

for example, "All metals expand if heated" is logically equivalent to "Anything that is either a raven or not a raven is either not a heated metal or it expands." Reichenbach will obviously want to exclude the implication which is the major operation of the latter statement from the class of reasonable operations even if the implication in the former statement is considered completely reasonable. In order to secure this sort of result, Reichenbach imposes the first V-requirement, 1.6, that p must be reduced. The additional three V-requirements, 1.7-1.9, serve to strengthen the reduction requirement in ways that need not be discussed in here.

I must now mention the third important difference between Reichenbach's new I-requirements for original nomological statements and those given in *Elements of Symbolic Logic*. Although the earlier explication required that original nomological statements be fully exhaustive, the later treatment relaxes that condition somewhat. The net result is that, in some cases, an original nomological statement may fail to be exhaustive in major terms. This makes it possible to say, in some cases, that an implication is reasonable when an equivalence can be asserted as original nomological, and that an inclusive disjunction is reasonable when an exclusive disjunction can be asserted as original nomological. This weakening seems to conform to common usage.

Having defined the class of original nomological statements in terms of the nine I- and V-requirements, Reichenbach can immediately define the class of *nomological statements* (or *nomological statements in the wider sense*) as the class of statements deducible from original nomological statements. Evidently the class of nomological statements contains the class of original nomological statements, since any statement is deducible from itself. As mentioned above, the class of nomological statements defines the modality of physical necessity. The modalities of physical possibility and physical impossibility are easily definable in terms of physical necessity. Thus, the theory of nomological statements has provided an explication of the physical modalities.

The remaining task is to explicate the concept of an *admissible statement* to serve as a basis for a definition of a "reasonable operation." Original nomological statements are admissible. Some, but not all, statements deducible from original nomological statements are admissible. We must see what restrictions are needed to define the class of admissible statements (or *nomological statements in the narrower sense*). This definition, it turns out, will have two parts; Reichenbach introduces both *fully admissible statements* and *semi-admissible statements*. The class of admissible statements contains both types.

The key to an understanding of the treatment of admissible statements is a hierarchy of orders of truth and falsity. Tautologies (logically or analytically true statements) are true of order 3. Synthetic nomological statements (original or derivative) are true of order 2. Verifiably true statements that are not nomological are true of order 1. The order of falsity of a statement $\bar{p}$ is equal to the order of truth of its contradictory p. Reichenbach's general strategy is to rule out, as inadmissible or "unreasonable," counterfactuals whose order of truth is not higher than the order of falsity of their antecedents.

Consider, for example, the statement, "If this table salt were placed in water, it would dissolve." The conditional statement is true of order 2, for it follows from law-statements. The falsity of the antecedent—that the salt was placed in water—is clearly of order 1, for its falsity is not a consequence of any law of nature. Similarly, the statement, "If light were not wavelike, then such diffraction phenomena as the Poisson bright spot would not occur," is admissible. The wavelike character of light is certainly nomological, so the antecedent of the conditional is false of order 2, but the conditional—which expresses a logical relationship—is true of order 3. The statement, "If Ohm's law were not true, then Newton's law of gravitation would not be true," is not an acceptable subjunctive conditional because its indicative counterpart, "If Ohm's law is not true then Newton's law of gravitation is not true," violates the condition on orders of truth and falsity. The conditional itself is true of order 2, for its truth follows from the truth of Ohm's law. The antecedent is also false of order 2, for its falsity follows from the same law. This example shows once more that the class of nomological statements (in the wider sense) is too broad to provide a satisfactory explication of admissible statements and admissible operations.

In this context, as in the treatment of original nomological statements, Reichenbach is concerned with all types of propositional operations, not just implications. In order to exploit the concept of orders of truth in defining a class of reasonable operations, he extends the concept of exhaustiveness. A general statement, it will be recalled, can be transformed into a prenex form in which all the operators stand at the front of the formula and have scopes extending to the end. The operand of all these operators can then be transformed into a disjunctive normal form. A residual of such a statement was defined as the statement that results from deletion of one or more terms of the disjunction (along with a suitable number of disjunction-symbols). The original statement was said to be exhaustive (in major terms or in elementary terms, depending on which type of disjunctive normal form was used) if none of its residuals is true. Reichenbach now offers the following definition:

A statement p which is true of order k is *quasi-exhaustive* (in major or in elementary terms) if none of its disjunctive residuals (in major or in elementary terms) is true of an order $\geq k$.[51]

Since a statement that has no true residuals obviously has no residuals true of an order $\geq k$, every exhaustive statement is also quasi-exhaustive.

Fully admissible statements are now defined in terms of a set of I-requirements and a set of V-requirements. The I-requirements are:

2.1 The statement p must be deductively derivable from a set of original nomological statements, i.e., p must be a nomological statement (in the wider sense).

2.2 The statement p must be quasi-exhaustive in elementary terms.[52]

Requirement 2.2 obviously rules out such unreasonable statements as "If Newton's law of gravitation holds, then Ohm's law of electric circuits is true," but it admits such reasonable conditionals as "If Newton's law of gravitation is true, then Kepler's law of planetary motion are true." The V-requirements for fully admissible statements are precisely the same as the V-requirements for original nomological statements. These, it will be recalled, had essentially the force of demanding that such statements be reduced—that is, free of redundancies.

Given the set of fully admissible statements—that is, statements that are nomological, quasi-exhaustive, and reduced—we might naturally ask whether these do not provide an adequate basis for the characterization of admissible operations. The answer, it turns out, is negative, as we can see by consideration of an example introduced earlier. If we assume that the statement, "All and only those animals that have hearts have kidneys," is original nomological, then "All animals with hearts have kidneys" is not original nomological, for it fails the test of exhaustiveness.[53] This latter statement is, of course, nomological in the wider sense, but that is not enough to insure that its major operation is reasonable. If this statement were admissible, the job would be done, but we can see immediately that it does not qualify as fully admissible because it is not quasi-exhaustive. The residual that results from the deletion of the term "x is an animal and x does not have a heart and x has a kidney" is true of order 2, which is the same order as the statement itself.[54] A definition of admissible statements which ruled out this statement would be unsatisfactory, for we would want to allow it to support the counterfactual, "If x were an animal with a heart then x would be an animal with a kidney." Thus we need to define the class of semi-admissible statements to include such examples among the class of admissible statements.

In providing the explication of semi-admissible statements, Reichenbach introduces the further concept of *supplementability*. A statement is supplementable, roughly, if it can be made a factor in a reduced conjunction that is equivalent to a fully admissible statement. The foregoing example obviously fulfills this condition. "All animals with hearts have kidneys" can be conjoined to "All animals with kidneys have hearts," and this conjunction (which is reduced) is equivalent to the fully admissible statement, "All and only animals with hearts have kidneys." The relationship between the inclusive and exclusive disjunction can be handled in the same way. A disjunction of the form $A \lor B$ which is in fact exclusive can be written as a conjunction of the form $(A \lor B) . (\overline{A} \lor \overline{B})$.

The admissible statements include those that are fully admissible or semi-admissible. The major operation of an admissible statement is an admissible operation. Such operations may occur in subjunctive or counterfactual conditionals as well as other types of statements, such as disjunctions, containing "reasonable" operations. Reichenbach is able to prove that his admissible operations, especially the implications, have a variety of desirable characteristics. In particular, if a pair of contrary implications of the forms $A \supset B$ and $A \supset \overline{B}$ are both true neither of them can be admissible (theorem 20).[55]

It should be emphatically reemphasized that the foregoing characterizations of Reichenbach's concepts of original nomological statements, nomological statements, and admissible statements are rough, inaccurate, and inexact. I have been trying merely to bring out what I take to be the most significant and intuitive features of his treatment. The reader who goes through the first five chapters of *Laws, Modalities, and Counterfactuals* (the chapters that contain these analyses) will encounter thirty-six definitions, thirteen requirements, and twenty-one theorems—many of which are complex and unfamiliar. It seems to me, however, that anyone who has a fairly clear grasp of the following concepts can understand with some degree of adequacy what Reichenbach is attempting to accomplish and how he goes about it.

For original nomological statements:

1. Verifiably true statement
2. Universal statement
3. All-statement
4. Exhaustive statement
5. Statement general in self-contained factors
6. Reduced statement

For admissible statements:

7. Order of truth (or falsity)
8. Quasi-exhaustive statement
9. Supplementable statement.

I have tried to say enough about these concepts to give an intuitive notion of their content and their function. Anyone who wants to achieve genuine understanding of Reichenbach's theory must—needless to say—study his precise formulations in detail and with care. My aim has been partly to provide some guidance and partly to furnish some motivation for this rather formidable task.

With the completion of Chapter V, the fundamental concepts have all been introduced and explicated. The remaining chapters contain some interesting extensions, but the reader who has mastered the content of the first five chapters will have no difficulty with the remaining ones. Two topics covered in these latter chapters are worthy of mention, however, because they bear upon certain misgivings that might have been aroused concerning Reichenbach's use of his hierarchy of orders of truth. In the first place, there seem to be cases in which one wishes to deal with counterfactuals in which some, but not all, laws of nature are suspended. Such cases could give rise to counterfactuals whose truth is of order 2, and whose antecedent is also false of order 2. Chapter VI shows how the present theory can be extended to handle such cases. In the second place, it would seem that many counterfactuals that we encounter in everyday life, whose antecedents are false of order 1, are themselves true only of order 1. "If it had not rained I would have gone on a picnic," for example, does not follow from any nomological statement alone. In Chapter VIII, Reichenbach develops in detail his theory of *relative nomological statements*, within which counterfactuals of this sort are straightforwardly handled.

Any reader who does take the pains to work through this complex treatment of laws, modalities, and reasonable operations (including counterfactuals) may well react with the protest, "But surely there must be an easier way!" Whether this is true, I do not know. It seems plausible to suppose that someone with a good deal of logical acumen and a fair amount of patience could significantly streamline Reichenbach's account, without materially changing its content. I believe this is an enterprise eminently worth undertaking by someone possessing the requisite skills. I do not know of any other approach to this set of problems which gives as much promise of success as does Reichenbach's. And whether Reichenbach's analysis turns out, upon careful examination and reflection, to be satisfactory or unsatisfactory, the major concepts listed above are surely important to anyone attempting to grapple with this set of problems.

Near the beginning of Chapter VIII of *Elements of Symbolic Logic*, Reichenbach sets out the program he intends to implement:

> We agree with Hume that physical necessity is translatable into statements about repeated concurrences, including the prediction that the same combination will occur in the future, without exception. 'Physically necessary' is expressible in terms of 'always'. However, we have to find out how this definition can be given without misinterpretation of the language of physics.[56]

Similar considerations apply to law statements and counterfactuals. Reichenbach carries through his analysis without invoking any mysterious "connections" between properties of the sort that Hume's critique so persuasively proscribed. Chisholm, in his classic article on counterfactuals, seems to suggest that the problems cannot be resolved without reinstating such "connections."[57] Reichenbach also avoids the postulation of myriad "possible worlds" of the sort David Lewis resorts to.[58] Although such worlds may be "accessible" in the abstract set-theoretic sense of the term, they are forever inaccessible to us for purposes of observation. Reichenbach would have abhorred such metaphysical fantasies. Unlike many modal logicians, Reichenbach tried to provide more than abstract set-theoretical constructions; he was attempting to construct concepts that would be applicable to physics. Moreover, Reichenbach's concept of *verifiability as true* rests upon much deeper and more secure inductive foundations than does Goodman's concept of *projectability* with its merely linguistic analysis in terms of "entrenchment."[59]

It is not my intention to try to pass judgment upon the adequacy of Reichenbach's results. I am inclined to think, as hinted above, that the whole theory could be considerably simplified. I also believe that his scale of degrees of truth is probably too crude; he, himself, suggested that a finer scale might be needed.[60] What I am attempting to show is that Reichenbach's treatment deserves serious study, in spite of its difficulty and complexity. If there were a simple alternative that manifestly provides an adequate account of laws, modalities, counterfactuals, and related concepts, then we might be justified in neglecting Reichenbach's theory. Since no such alternative account does exist, it seems reasonable to take the trouble to learn what we can from Reichenbach's penetrating work. It certainly does not deserve the virtually total neglect it has received from authors currently writing on these topics.

NOTES

1. A good general survey of work in modal logic can be found in G.E. Hughes and M.J. Cresswell, *An Introduction to Modal Logic* (London: Methuen and Co. Ltd, 1968).

2. David Lewis, *Counterfactuals* (Cambridge, Mass.: Harvard University Press, 1973), p. 85.

3. *Ibid.*, p. 88.

4. This point applies equally to "inductive logic," if there is such a thing, for it cannot make a single step in this direction without the aid of concrete empirical evidence.

5. The recent book by the Italian physicist, Aldo Bressan, *A General Interpreted Modal Calculus* (New Haven: Yale University Press, 1972), is *the* striking exception. It was apparently undertaken precisely in order to deal with problems in the logical foundation of physics, and it was evidently done completely independently of the work of logicians in the mainstream of modal logic. Whether Bressan's development of modal logic will shed light on the nature of physical necessity I am not prepared to say. However, this work is considered by Nuel Belnap—a leading authority in the field of modal logic—to represent a breakthrough of significant proportions. See Belnap's Foreword to this book.

6. David Lewis, *Counterfactuals*, pp. 5-7, makes explicit use of physical laws in characterizing physical possibility, but he provides no analysis of laws.

7. Alan Ross Anderson and Nuel D. Belnap, Jr., *Entailment. The Logic of Relevance and Necessity*, Vol. I (Princeton, N.J.: Princeton University Press, 1975).

8. G.H. von Wright is a distinguished contributor; see his *An Essay in Deontic Logic and the General Theory of Action* (Amsterdam: North-Holland Publishing Co., 1968).

9. A.N. Prior's *Time and Modality* (Oxford: Clarendon Press, 1957) and *Past, Present and Future* (Oxford: Clarendon Press, 1968) are well-known works in this area.

10. See A.N. Prior, "Logic, Modal," in *The Encyclopedia of Philosophy*, ed. Paul Edwards (New York: Macmillan Publishing Co., 1967), V:5-12.

11. C.G. Hempel and Paul Oppenheim, "Studies in the Logic of Explanation," originally published in *Philosophy of Science*, 15 (1948), 135-175. Reprinted, with a 1964 Postscript in Carl G. Hempel, *Aspects of Scientific Explanation* (New York: The Free Press, 1965), pp. 245-295.

12. See the 1964 Postscript, pp. 291-295, mentioned in n. 11.

13. Nelson Goodman, *Fact, Fiction, and Forecast* (Cambridge, Mass.: Harvard University Press, 1955); reprinted with revisions (Indianapolis: The Bobbs-Merrill Co., 1965).

14. The choice of this particular example is unfortunate. My dictionary makes the color green a defining property of emeralds, thus rendering the first of these two generalizations analytic. Synthetic examples are, however, easily devised.

15. See the following exchange between Goodman and Carnap: Nelson Goodman, "A Query on Confirmation," *Journal of Philosophy*, xliii (1946), 383-385; Rudolf Carnap, "On the Application of Inductive Logic," *Philosophy and Phenomenological Research*, 8 (1947); Nelson Goodman, "On Infirmities of Confirmation Theory," *Philosophy and Phenomenological Research*, 8 (1947), 149-151; Rudolf Carnap, "Reply to Nelson Goodman," *Philosophy and Phenomenological Research* 8 (1947), 461-462.

16. It is a little known fact that Bertrand Russell in *Human Knowledge: Its Scope and Limits* (New York: Simon and Schuster, 1948), pp. 404-405, actually stated and offered a plausible resolution of this problem. My attempt at resolution, which I still consider fundamentally sound, is given in "On Vindicating Induction," *Philosophy of Science*, 30, 3 (July 1963), 252-261, esp. pp. 256 ff. Also published in Henry E. Kyburg, Jr., and Ernest Nagel, eds., *Induction: Some Current Issues* (Middletown, Conn.: Wesleyan University Press, 1963), pp. 27-44.

17. In the 1964 Postscript to a classic article on confirmation, *Aspects of Scientific Explanation*, pp. 47-51, Hempel acknowledges the significance of Goodman's problem as it bears upon confirmation. He might have noted its bearing on explanation as a corollary.

18. Carl G. Hempel, *Philosophy of Natural Science* (Englewood Cliffs, N.J.: Prentice-Hall, Inc., 1966), p. 55. Reichenbach cites a similar example in the present book (p. 11).

19. See Benson Mates, *Elementary Logic*, 2d ed. (New York: Oxford University Press, 1972), pp. 212-214.

20. Roderick M. Chisholm, "The Contrary-to-Fact Conditional," *Mind*, 55 (1946), 289-307; Nelson Goodman, "The Problem of Counterfactual Conditionals," *Journal of Philosophy*, 44 (1947), 113-128. Both of these articles have been frequently reprinted.

21. Nelson Goodman, *Fact, Fiction, and Forecast*, 2d ed. (Indianapolis: The Bobbs-Merrill Co., 1965), p. x.

22. *Ibid.*, pp. ix-x.

23. For further references see Ernest Sosa, ed., *Causation and Conditionals* (Oxford: Oxford University Press, 1975), a recent anthology of essays on this topic. In this book Reichenbach's final chapter of *Elements of Symbolic Logic* rates one brief mention in a footnote, while *Nomological Statements and Admissible Operations* is totally ignored.

24. Rudolf Carnap, "Testability and Meaning" *Philosophy of Science*, III (1936), 420-471; IV (1937), 2-40. Reprinted, with corrigenda and additional bibliography, by the Graduate Philosophy Club (New Haven, Conn.: Yale University, 1950).

25. See Carl G. Hempel, "A Logical Appraisal of Operationism," *Scientific Monthly* 79 (1954), 215-220. Reprinted, with slight revision, in *idem, Aspects of Scientific Explanation,* pp. 123-133.

26. Hans Reichenbach, *Elements of Symbolic Logic* (New York: The Macmillan Co., 1947) (Hereafter cited as ESL).

27. *Ibid.,* pp. 27-34. Reichenbach uses the term "operation" for negation, conjunction, disjunction, implication, and equivalence. These are often called "connectives" in the contemporary literature. I shall follow his terminology here, for as we are about to see, his introduces the term "connective operation." It would be awkward to alter his terminology and refer to "connective connectives."

28. *Ibid.*

29. *Ibid.,* pp. 368-369. I shall alter Reichenbach's order of presentation.

30. It would be more accurate to say that they qualify as derivative laws if suitable well-known corrections are made.

31. Reichenbach uses a bar over the top of a formula as a symbol for negation.

32. ESL., p. 363. "All animals with a heart have a kidney" will qualify as a derivative nomological statement; it is, so to speak, a derived law.

33. The "basic laws of logic"—as represented by analytic original nomological statements—will not correspond with those statements usually taken as axioms of standard logical systems.

34. P. 18.

35. ESL, p. 360.

36. ESL, p. 368.

37. Reichenbach, *The Theory of Probability* (Berkeley and Los Angeles: University of California Press, 1949), pp. 448-449.

38. Wesley C. Salmon, "On Vindicating Induction."

39. Pp. 11-12.

40. Reichenbach, *The Philosophy of Space and Time* (New York: Dover Publications, Inc., 1958), sect. 23, "Unreal Sequences."

41. Obviously the term *"C"* which effects the restriction must not contain explicit or implicit reference to *"B"*. *"C"* must function somewhat as a "place selection" in the sense of Richard von Mises.

42. I have tried to clarify this approach in my *Foundations of Scientific Inference* (Pittsburgh: University of Pittsburgh Press, 1967), Chap. VII.

43. ESL, p. 369.

44. See, for example, Definitions 15-16 and Requirement 1.5.

45. ESL, p. 368.

46. Definition 13.

47. See definition 14. At no place in Chap. III does Reichenbach offer an example of an original nomological statement with an initial existential operator.

48. Karl Popper would, I should think, deny even derivative nomological status to such statements, but he has given little attention to statements of mixed quantification.

49. P. 49.

50. P. 56.

51. P. 67.

52. *Ibid.*

53. I mentioned above that *some* implications can qualify as original nomological even if the corresponding equivalence is true, but the present example is not one which qualifies.

54. Pp. 69-70.

55. P. 81.

56. ESL, p. 356.

57. Chisholm, "Contrary-to-Fact Conditional."

58. David Lewis, *Counterfactuals.*

59. Goodman, *Fact, Fiction, and Forecast,* Chap. IV.

60. P. 83.

I

INTRODUCTION

The problem of a 'reasonable' implication has frequently occupied logicians. Whereas in conversational language this kind of propositional operation is regarded as having a clear and well-defined meaning, logicians have been compelled to define as implication a term of much wider meaning; and it appears extremely difficult to go back from this implication in a wider sense to the narrower and very specific meaning assumed for implication in a non-formalized language. We face here a discrepancy between usage and rules: whereas in actual usage everyone is quite able to say whether an implication is reasonable, he would be at a loss to give rules which distinguish reasonable implications from unreasonable ones. The term 'reasonable', therefore, is a challenge to the logician for finding rules delineating a usage that follows unconscious rules.

The problem of uncovering such rules appears even more difficult when it is realized that 'reasonable' implications of conversational language are not restricted to implications expressing a *logical entailment*, but include what may be called a *physical entailment*. For the first kind, we may use as an illustration the implication, 'if all men are mortal and Socrates is a man, then Socrates is mortal'. The second kind may be illustrated by the implication, 'if a metal is heated, it expands'. Since the latter kind of implication expresses what is called a law of nature, whereas the former may be said to express a law of logic, I have proposed to include both kinds under the name of *nomological* implications.

It is easily seen that the problem under consideration is not specific for implication, but concerns all propositional operations alike. The 'or', for instance, can have an 'unreasonable' as well as a 'reasonable' meaning. To say, 'snow is white or sugar is sour', appears as unreasonable as saying 'if snow is not white, sugar is sour'; but both statements are true in the sense of the operations defined in the truth tables of symbolic logic. A reasonable 'or' would be given in the statement: 'there is sufficient rain in the winter or there is a drought in the summer', an exclusive disjunction which for many a country expresses a consequential alternative. Since the operation is made reasonable by the compound statement whose major operation it is and which expresses a law of nature or of logic, we face here the general problem of *nomological statements*, a class of statements which subdivides into the two subclasses of analytic and synthetic nomological statements. The statement confers a certain prerogative upon its major operation, which may be called a *nomological operation*. It will be seen, however, that the operations so defined are still too general to supply 'reasonable' propositional operations, and that such operations must be defined as a subclass of nomological operations.

Based on these considerations, I have developed in an earlier presentation [1] a theory of nomological statements. Since we are here concerned with an *explication* of a term, i.e., with constructing a precise term proposed to take over the functions of a vague term, we cannot expect to arrive at results which cover the usage of the vague term without exceptions; if only for the reason that the vague term is used differently by different persons. All that can be achieved, therefore, is constructing a formal definition which corresponds to the usage of the vague term at least in a high percentage of cases. For this reason, I thank those of my critics who have drawn my attention to cases where there appears to be a discrepancy between *explicans* and *explicandum*, if these terms are used to denote the precise term and the vague term, respectively. To their criticisms, I added my own and found more such discrepancies. In the present monograph, I wish to develop an improved definition of laws of nature and reasonable operations, hoping that the percentage of cases of adequate interpretation is thus increased. For the remaining cases, my definition may be regarded as a proposal for future usage of the term, and I should be glad if it

---

[1] In my book, *Elements of Symbolic Logic*, New York, 1947, chap. VIII. This book will be quoted as ESL.

appears possible to adjust one's own usage to the proposed definition without sacrificing essential connotations.

In its fundamental idea, the new theory corresponds to the old one; and I will therefore give here a short summary of the older theory insofar as it is taken over into the present one. The truth tables of symbolic logic represent metalinguistic statements expressing relations between compound statements of the object language and their elementary statements. Now these tables can be read in two directions. Going from the compound statement to the elementary statements, we read the tables as a disjunction of T-cases, for instance, as follows:

First direction. If '$a \supset b$' is true, then 'a' is true and 'b' is true, or 'a' is false and 'b' is true, or 'a' is false and 'b' is false.

Going from the elementary statements to the compound statement, we read the tables as follows:

Second direction. If 'a' is true and 'b' is true, then '$a \supset b$' is true. If 'a' is false and 'b' is true, then '$a \supset b$' is true. If 'a' is false and 'b' is false, then '$a \supset b$' is true.

In the interpretation assumed for mathematical logic, both directions of reading are used. I speak here of an *adjunctive* interpretation of the truth tables and, correspondingly, of *adjunctive operations*. [1] It is possible, however, to omit the second direction of reading the truth tables and to use only the first direction. I then speak of a *connective* interpretation of the truth tables and, correspondingly, of *connective operations*.

It is important to realize that, for all 'reasonable' operations of conversational language, the truth tables are adequate if we read them only in the first direction, i.e., interpret these operations as connective. Deviations from a reasonable usage occur only when, in addition, the tables are read in the second direction. In other words, reasonable operations are not adjunctive, but connective.

For instance, consider the reasonable implication: 'If a large sun spot turns up on the day of the concert, the short-wave radio

---

[1] The term 'adjunctive' corresponds to such terms as 'extensional', 'truth-functional', 'material', which have been used in presentations of logic. But since these terms are often used in various meanings, I prefer to use the precisely defined term 'adjunctive'.

transmission of the concert will be seriously disturbed'. When we regard this statement as true, before the concert is given, we shall be quite willing to admit that any of the three possible cases stated for the first direction may occur. However, we would refuse to regard the statement as verified if, say, no sun spot turns up and the short-wave radio-transmission of the concert is not disturbed; and we would not even be willing to regard the implication as verified even if a sun spot turns up and the radio transmission is disturbed, unless further evidence for a causal relation between the two phenomena is adduced. [1] This means that we use here a connective implication, but not an adjunctive implication. Similar examples are easily given for the other propositional operations.

It follows that a definition of reasonable operations cannot be achieved by changing the truth tables. These tables are adequate; however, we have to renounce the use of the second direction for reading the tables. This program can be carried out as follows. We define connective operations as a subclass of the corresponding adjunctive operations. Then, whenever a connective operation is true, the corresponding adjunctive operation is also true, and the use of the first direction of reading the truth tables is thus assured. However, the second direction is excluded, because a verification of compound connective statements requires more than a verification of the corresponding adjunctive statement. In other words, satisfying the requirement for an adjunctive operation is merely a necessary, not a sufficient condition for the verification of the corresponding connective operation.

Connective operations will be defined as nomological operations, i.e., as major operations of nomological statements. In a nomological statement, all propositional operations are used, first, in the adjunctive sense; i.e., the statement must be true in an adjunctive interpretation. But in addition, the statement has to satisfy certain requirements of another kind. The introduction of suitable

---

[1] The case that 'a' is true and 'b' is true is sometimes regarded as verifying a reasonable implication, sometimes, however, as insufficient for a verification. If this case is regarded as verifying the implication, I speak of a semi-adjunctive implication. See ESL, § 64.

requirements of this kind constitutes the problem of the present investigation.

As far as analytic nomological statements are concerned, the method outlined here has found an application in Carnap's theory of analytic implication. Carnap has pointed out that if an implication stands in the place of the major operation of a tautology or analytic statement, it can be regarded as an explicans for the relation of logical entailment. This conception will be taken over into the present theory. However, what is to be added is a corresponding definition for physical entailment, and with it, quite generally, for synthetic nomological statements. Furthermore, it will be shown, as mentioned above, that the class of nomological operations is still too wide to supply what may be called 'reasonable' operations. This applies both to the synthetic and to the analytic case; in fact, not all tautological implications appear reasonable. For instance, the tautological implication, '$a . \bar{a} \supset b$', can scarcely be accepted as reasonable.

The general form of the theory to be developed, which is the same as the form of my previous theory, can now be outlined as follows. First, a class of *original nomological statements* is defined; then the class of *nomological statements* is constructed as comprising all those statements that are deductively derivable from sets of statements of the first class. Among these, a narrower group is defined as *nomological in the narrower sense*. It is this group, also called the group of *admissible statements*, which is regarded as supplying reasonable propositional operations, while the class of nomological statements supplies the laws of nature and the laws of logic. As in the previous theory, the original nomological statements are included in the admissible statements. Furthermore, analytic, or tautological, statements are included in nomological statements, a subclass of them being admissible, as in the older theory. The new definitions replace § 61 and § 63 in ESL; the other sections of chapter VIII in ESL remain unchanged. As in ESL, the theory is developed only for the simple calculus of functions. An extension to the higher calculus can presumably be constructed, but would require further investigation.

Although the class of 'reasonable' operations must be defined as a narrower subclass of nomological operations, one must not conclude that the latter operations appear completely 'unreasonable'. It seems that there is no unique explicans for the term 'reasonable'; the requirements which we tacitly include in this term differ with the context in which the operation is used. The theory presented accounts for these variations by defining various categories and indicating their specific characteristics and applications.

As an instrument for carrying out this construction, a distinction between three orders of truth is introduced. Analytic truth supplies the highest, or third order, synthetic nomological truth the second order, and merely factual truth the lowest, or first order. The two higher orders of truth, which constitute *nomological truth* and embrace all nomological statements, are thus set above merely *factual truth*. This distinction is used, in turn, for the definition of nomological statements in the narrower sense, which are constructed in such a way that if their essential parts are true taken separately, they are true of a lower order than the statement itself. By means of this method, certain rather strong requirements of reasonableness can be satisfied.

An important application of nomological statements in the wider sense is given by the definition of *modalities*. These categories are not presupposed for nomological statements, but are defined by their help and constitute a sort of byproduct of the theory of nomological statements. The modalities are usually referred, not to a statement, but to the situation, or state of affairs, denoted by it; i.e., they are used in the object language. We thus define:

a is necessary if 'a' is nomological.

a is impossible if '$\bar{a}$' is nomological.

a is merely possible (contingent) if neither 'a' nor '$\bar{a}$' is nomological.

For 'merely possible', the term 'possible' is often used, but sometimes 'possible' refers to the disjunction of 'necessary' and 'merely possible'. It can easily be seen that the term 'nomological' of these definitions must be interpreted as nomological in the wider sense; if we attempted to interpret it as nomological in the narrower sense, we would be led into serious difficulties. For instance, certain analytic statements would then not describe necessary situations. Whereas the use of analytic statements for the definition of *logical modalities* is obvious, it is the significance of the given definitions that they also allow for the definition of *physical modalities*. These two kinds of modalities result according as, in the above definitions, the term 'nomological' is specified as analytic or synthetic nomological, respectively. Furthermore, a distinction between absolute and relative modalities must be made; for these points and the further theory of modalities I refer to ESL, § 65. In the following presentation, we shall occasionally refer to modalities for the purpose of illustrating nomological statements.

The class of admissible implications is constructed for the purpose of satisfying very strong requirements and thus of explicating reasonable implications in the narrowest sense of the term. Conversational language has two kinds of usage for implications subject to very exacting requirements: they are used for predictions, or they are employed as conditionals contrary to fact. It is obvious that adjunctive implications cannot convey important information in a *predictive usage*. In order to know that the implication is true, we would have to know that a particular T-case, which verifies it, is true; but once we know this T-case, we would lose in information if we merely state the implication and not the T-case itself. This applies whether we know the truth of the T-case from past observations or because we can predict it. For instance, we can predict that it will be Wednesday tomorrow and that the sun will rise; replacing this conjunction by the adjunctive implication, 'if it is Wednesday tomorrow the sun will rise', we say less than we know, and therefore such an implication has no practical use.

It has often been emphasized that for a *counterfactual usage*, likewise, adjunctive implications are completely inadequate. Nobody would say, 'if snow were not white, sugar would be sour', although this implication is true in the adjunctive sense. But we would say, 'if this metal were heated, it would expand'. Since conversational language is rather clear and unambiguous in the usage of conditionals contrary to fact, we possess in this usage a sensitive test for the adequacy of the explication of reasonable implications, and we shall often make use of it. For instance, it is required for a conditional contrary to fact that it be unique. By this property I mean that, if the implication '$a \supset b$' is used for a conditional contrary to fact, the contrary implication '$a \supset \bar{b}$' cannot be so used. Obviously, adjunctive implication does not satisfy the condition of uniqueness when it is used counterfactually, because, if 'a' is false, both contrary implications are true in the adjunctive sense. It has often been pointed out that this absence of uniqueness makes adjunctive implications inappropriate for counterfactual use. In the theory of admissible implications it will therefore be an important requirement that two contrary implications cannot be both admissible. The present theory satisfies this requirement, whereas my previous theory could satisfy it only to some extent.

Since the theory to be developed is rather technical and involves much detail, the significance of which is at first not easily seen, it may be advisable to outline the major ideas on which the definition of original nomological statements is based. These ideas have been developed essentially for synthetic nomological statements, because statements of this kind are in the foreground of this investigation; the application to tautologies is then rather easily given.

The leading idea in the definition of original nomological statements of the synthetic kind will, of course, be given by the principle that such statements must be general statements, or all-statements, and must not be restricted to a single case. We know from the writings of David Hume that physical necessity, the necessity of the laws of nature, springs from generality, that causal connection differs from mere coincidence in that it expresses a permanence of the coincidence. Hume believed that this generality is all that is required for causal connection. He was right when he insisted that unverifiable additions to this requirement should be ruled out; in fact, any belief in hidden ties between cause and effect represents a surplus meaning which Occam's razor would shave away. However, it turns out that generality alone, though necessary, is not sufficient to guarantee that all unreasonable forms are ruled out. We shall therefore introduce, in addition to generality, a set of requirements restricting the statement forms to be admitted. It goes without saying that these additions are formulated as verifiable properties of statements, and that, for a given statement, we can always find out whether it satisfies the requirements.

In his early writings on mathematical logic, Bertrand Russell has pointed out that a general implication of the form, '$(x)[f(x) \supset g(x)]$' eliminates the unreasonable properties of adjunctive implication to some extent, but that these properties reappear if the implicans '$f(x)$' is always false or the implicate '$g(x)$' is always true. The exclusion of these two cases will therefore be an important requirement within the definition of a reasonable implication. However, for a general theory of nomological statements, this requirement must be generalized so as to be applicable likewise to other operations and to statements possessing several operators, among which there may be existential operators. It can be shown that for the latter case an implicans which is not always false does not exclude an unreasonable implication. The construction of such a more comprehensive requirement is achieved by means of a formal property of statements, which is called *exhaustiveness* and which will be defined in group E of chapter 2. (See also the discussion of (40a–b) in chapter 3.)

Even if an implication satisfies the requirements so far mentioned, it can have forms that are not accepted as reasonable. Assume that during a certain time it so happens that all persons in a certain room are over 30 years old; then the general implication, 'for all x, if x is a person in this room at this time, x is over 30 years old', is true in the adjunctive sense, and its implicans is not always false. Yet this implication does not appear reasonable, as is seen when it is used counterfactually: the statement, 'if another person had been in this room at this time, he would have been over 30 years old', would not be acceptable as true. This example shows that a reasonable implication has to satisfy further requirements, which exclude a restriction of the implication to certain times and places and guarantee its *universal* application. These requirements will be explained in group F, chapter 2.

It should be noted that requirements of this kind are rather strong and are adhered to, in conversational language, only when the implicational character of the statement is explicitly stated, for instance by using terms like 'if-then', 'implies', etc. No objection, however, is raised when the statement is given the wording: 'all persons in this room at this time were over 30 years old', which form appears quite reasonable. In the disguise of a conversational all-statement, therefore, we accept adjunctive implications, a fact which shows that these implications are not merely a creation of the logician but are widely used in conversational language. The present investigation into the nature of reasonable implications is therefore restricted to an explicit use of this operation. Similar considerations apply to other propositional operations.

It turns out that in order to carry through the requirements mentioned it is necessary to introduce rules which eliminate redundant parts of statements and define a procedure of *reduction*, by means of which a statement is transformed into simpler forms. This is necessary, first, because a reasonable statement could easily be made unreasonable by adding to it redundant parts; for instance, if a statement contains no terms referring to a particular space-time region, we could add to it some tautology containing such terms without changing the meaning of the statement. [1] Secondly, however, it may be possible to insert parts that are merely factually true into a nomological statement in such a way that the statement still satisfies the requirements mentioned previously. In combination with certain other requirements, the reduction procedure rules out such forms; and I have been able to construct a proof that unreasonable parts of a certain kind cannot be contained in original nomological statements as defined in this presentation (see theorem 5).

All the criteria so far mentioned are of a formal nature; and they are based on the assumption that we are able to find out whether these formal relations hold. For instance, it is presupposed that we are able to find out whether a statement is equipollent to a given other statement, whether it can be written in syntactical forms of a certain kind, such as an all-statement, etc. In as much as such

---

[1] This objection was raised correctly against my previous theory by J. C. C. McKinsey, *American Mathematical Monthly*, vol. 55, 1948, pp. 261–263; and by N. Goodman, Philos. Review 1948, vol. 57, pp. 100–102.

an assumption is made, the present theory presupposes the completeness of the lower functional calculus. However, since a general decision procedure cannot be constructed for this calculus, we cannot give rules indicating how the test for equipollence is to be made. In principle, therefore, there may exist statements of complicated forms for which we are actually unable to decide whether they satisfy the requirements laid down; we then have to put these statements into a category under the heading, 'at present unknown whether nomological', and hope that some day they will be taken out of this category, because in principle the decision can be made. In practice, however, we shall encounter no such difficulties, because scientific laws have rather simple syntactical forms and cannot compete, as to structural form, with the involved statements which the mathematical logician likes to make the subject of his investigation.

From formal properties I will now turn to the discussion of a property which is independent of form. Being laws of nature, nomological statements, of course, must be true; they must even be *verifiably true*, which is a stronger requirement than truth alone. Some remarks about this requirement must now be added. [1]

The requirement of truth is not sufficient because we wish to exclude from nomological statements those all-statements which are merely factually true, or 'true by chance'. This kind of statement may obtain even if no reference to individual space-time regions is made; for instance, the statement, 'all gold cubes are smaller than one cubic mile', may possibly be true. When we reject a statement of this kind as not expressing a law of nature, we mean to say that observable facts do not require any such statement for their interpretation and thus do not confer any truth, or any degree of probability, on it. If they did, if we had good inductive evidence for the statement, we would be willing to accept it. For instance, the statement, 'all signals are slower than

---

[1] In ESL, p. 369, I used the term 'demonstrably true'. Since 'demonstrable' usually refers only to deductive proof, I will now use the above term. The term 'verifiable' alone would not suffice because it is now generally used in the neutral meaning 'verifiable as true or false'.

or equally fast as light signals', is accepted as a law of nature because observable facts confer a high probability upon it. It is the inductive verification, not mere truth, which makes an all-statement a law of nature. In fact, if we could prove that gold cubes of giant size would condense under gravitational pressure into a sun-like gas ball whose atoms were all disintegrated, we would be willing also to accept the statement about gold cubes among the laws of nature.

The reason is easily explained. The inductive inference extends truth from 'some' to 'all'; it therefore allows for a predictive as well as counterfactual use of implications. We saw that these two kinds of usage are essential for reasonable implications; therefore, if an implication is inductively verified, it qualifies for the category of reasonable implications. We discussed the example of an implication which is restricted to persons in a certain room during a certain time; when we reject such an implication for counterfactual use, it is because this implication is not verified through inductive extension. The requirement that the all-statement be verifiably true, therefore, guarantees the kind of truth with which we wish to establish laws of nature; it guarantees *inductive generality*.

The word 'verifiable' includes a reference to possibility. Since physical possibility is a category to be defined in terms of nomological statements, it would be circular to use, in the definition of such statements, this category. For this reason, I defined the term 'verifiably true' as meaning verified at some time, in the past or in the future. It has been argued against this definition that there may be laws of nature which will never be discovered by human beings. [1] In the present investigation I shall show that the latter statement, indeed, can be given a meaning, and that we can define a term *verifiably true in the wider sense* which covers this meaning. But in order to define this term, I shall begin with the narrower

---

[1]   This objection was raised against my theory in a letter by Mr. Albert Hofstadter, which included some further interesting objections answered in the present paper. The same objection was made by G. D. W. Berry, *Journ. of Symbolic Logic*, vol. 14, 1949, p. 52.

term, and proceed later to the introduction of the wider term (chapter 6).

Although inductive verifiability is presupposed for nomological statements, the definition of such statements can be given without entering into an analysis of the methods of verification. What we are looking for in a definition of nomological statements is not a method of verifying such statements, but a set of rules which guarantee that inductive verification is actually used for these statements, in as much as they are synthetic. The requirements laid down in the definition of nomological statements, in fact, represent a set of restrictions which exclude from such statements all synthetic forms that can be verified without inductive extension. More than that, the restrictions single out, among inductively verified statements, a special group of all-statements associated with a very high degree of probability; and they are so constructed that they allow us to assume that these all-statements are true without exceptions. Merely factual truth, though in itself found by inductive inference, is thus distinguished from nomological truth in that it does not assert an inductive generality; and the requirements introduced for nomological statements are all governed by the very principle that factual truth must never be sufficient to verify deductively a statement of this kind.

The predictive usage of admissible implications is thus reduced to the predictive use of inductive inferences equipped with high degrees of probability. Their counterfactual usage, likewise, appears justified by this interpretation, although this usage imposes even stronger requirements upon implications than a predictive usage, as will be shown in chapter 7. It is its origin in inductive extension, its inductive generality, that makes an implication reasonable.

Since the function of the requirements to be introduced is thus negative rather than positive, inasmuch as these requirements are merely restrictive, it is not necessary to give in this presentation a detailed discussion of inductive verification. That inductive methods exist and are applied, is a familiar fact; their study belongs in a theory of induction and probability, and as far as my own conception of this subject matter is concerned, I refer to another

publication. [1] However, I should like to add to the present investigation a brief account of the methods of inductive verification
in their relation to general implication; this account is given in
the appendix.

Those who have studied the construction of artificial languages
are often sceptical as to the possibility of finding rules that govern
conversational language. They are disappointed by the vagueness
of the terms used in the language of everyday life, and point to
the apparent inconsistencies in actual usage of language. Yet on
closer inspection, it turns out that a natural language is by no
means as inconsistent as is sometimes believed. If it is difficult to
find rules, one must not conclude that no rules exist. Physical
phenomena, too, do not always openly display the rules followed
by them; but physicists have been able to show that all such
phenomena are controlled by very precise rules, though the
formulation of these rules may be extremely complicated. A natural
language is a complex system of psychological and sociological
phenomena, and one cannot expect its laws to be visible to the
untrained eye. Those who are not afraid to search for its laws,
however, have been surprised to discover that rather precise laws
can be constructed into actual usage of language, and that, once
laws have been abstracted from single examples, they cover large
parts of usage practically without exceptions.

Perhaps it is possible to explain the hidden precision of language
by the fact that language behavior is continuously tested and
corrected by its practical applications; that, in particular, predictions and conditionals contrary to fact are of greatest significance
in everyday life, and that a language which were inexact in the
use of such concepts would soon be led into serious conflicts with
observational experiences. If it is required for a reasonable implication to be applicable to predictions, the usage of reasonable
implications is not a matter of taste, or of social convention, but
something eminently practical; and if we have developed a natural

---

[1]   To my book, *The Theory of Probability*, second edition, Berkeley 1949;
quoted as ThP. This book includes a discussion of induction for predictive
usage and a justification of induction, problems which cannot be dealt with
in the present monograph.

feeling for the reasonableness of an implication, we have been so conditioned by the exigencies of everyday life. Thus practical needs have made language a forceful instrument which owes its efficiency to its precision. The study of natural languages, therefore, offers to the logician the possibility of making laws explicit which, though unknown to the language user, implicitly control his language behavior and make it consistent. The present study is intended to be a contribution to this task.

II

FUNDAMENTAL TERMS

In the definition of nomological statements we shall refer to two kinds of properties of these statements. First, we shall speak of properties which remain invariant for tautological, or equipollent, transformations, such as truth, or being synthetic. These will be called *invariant properties*. Terms used for the formulation of these properties will be called *I-terms*. Second, we shall speak of properties which a statement has only in a particular form of writing, and which do not remain invariant for all tautological, or equipollent, transformations, such as being an implication, or containing an all-operator. These will be called *variant properties*. Terms used for the formulation of such properties will be called *V-terms*. The definition of nomological statements will be laid down in certain requirements, which we distinguish correspondingly as *I-requirements* and *V-requirements*.

In the beginning, we shall deal only with original nomological statements. For their definition both kinds of requirements will be used. The term 'original nomological' is thus made a *V*-term. In order to construct the requirements, it is advisable first to define certain terms which are to be used. These definitions are ordered by groups.

Notational remark. Sentence name variables, belonging to the metalanguage, will be expressed by the letters 'p', 'q', 'r', etc; combinations of such letters will be interpreted in the sense of autonymous use of operations (Carnap), such that '$p.q$' is the name of the conjunction of p and q. Sentential variables, belonging in the object language, will be expressed by the letters 'a', 'b', 'c', etc.; functional and argument variables, likewise belonging in the object language, will be expressed by the letters 'f', 'g', 'x', 'y', etc. These variables require the use of quotation marks within a continuous text; for formulae on separate lines the quotation marks will be omitted. Likewise, quotation marks will be omitted after a colon in the text.

The metalinguistic variables will be used when reference is made to the inner structure of the sentences denoted by the individual letters. The object language variables will be used, first, when no reference is made to the inner structure of the sentence, or the function, abbreviated by one letter, and all the structure referred to is expressed by combination of letters. Secondly, however, object language variables will be used in a mixed context, where the structure of the sentences is partially expressed, partially described in words.

The distinction between these cases may be illustrated by examples. I shall write: 'a' is derivable from '$a.b$'; the variable 'x' in '$(x)f(x)$' is bound; etc. In these cases, no reference is made to the inner structure of the expressions abbreviated by one letter, and the truth of the metalinguistic sentence is visible from the structure expressed by the symbols. In contrast, reference to inner structure of the individual sentences referred to is made in such statements as, 'p is derivable from q', for which I use metalinguistic variables. The truth of such a statement is not visible from the structure indicated by the symbols; therefore such statements can only occur in conditional form, such as: if p is derivable from q, then ...; assume that p is nomological; etc. A mixed context is given by a statement of the form: if '$f(x) \supset g(x)$' is analytic and 'f' is not identical with 'g', then 'f' or 'g' is composed of elementary functions. If such statements were formulated by the help of metalinguistic variables, autonymous use would have to be extended to the parentheses; although this could of course be consistently done, I prefer to use object language variables and quotes. The decision for one or the other method is a matter of style and personal taste, not of correctness. Those who do not like the rather wide use of quotes may regard the expression, ''f' is composed of elementary functions', as an abbreviation for the longer expression, ''f' is interpreted by a function which is composed of elementary functions'. Likewise, the expression, ''a' is an implication', can be regarded as an abbreviation for the longer expression, ''a' is interpreted by an implication'. In this way, the wider use of quotes can be regarded as an abbreviated mode of speech translatable into a narrower use of quotes. Note that the wider use of quotes can occur only in conditional sentences.

In a synthetic statement, sentential and functional variables express uninterpreted constants, i.e., such statements are true only for specific values of these variables. In an analytic statement, sentential and functional variables represent free variables in the sense that any value may be given to them while the statement remains true. A notational distinction between these two cases will not be made, because the same letter may represent a free variable for the whole formula and an uninterpreted constant for a part of it. Bound functional variables will not be used since the presentation remains entirely within the lower functional calculus.

A sentence is called an elementary propositional term if it has no inner structure expressible by the use of propositional symbols; otherwise it is called compound. A function together with its variables, such as '$f(x, y)$', is called a functional. [1] A function is called elementary if it does not stand for a combination of other functions; otherwise it is called compound. A notational distinction between elementary and compound terms will not be made; in fact, owing to the vagueness of conversational language, such a distinction can scarcely be carried out uniquely. However, it is usually sufficient to assume that, in a certain context, some rule has been introduced laying down this distinction; the rule itself is irrelevant. Furthermore, if by regarding certain terms as elementary, a statement can be shown to be tautological, or to be derivable from some other statement, these relations will not be changed if the assumed elementary terms are further subdivided.

GROUP A. TRUTH AND TRANSFORMATIONS

Definition 1. A statement is *verifiably true* if it is verified as practically true at some time during the past, present, or future history of mankind. (*I*-term).

If a statement is regarded as verified at some time, but regarded as falsified at a later time, then the later decision takes precedence,

---

[1]   ESL, p. 81.

being based on a more comprehensive body of evidence. The earlier decision is regarded as erroneous.

Definition 2. When we say that a statement p *can be written as p'* or that *p is equisignificant to p'*, it is meant that p and p' contain certain elementary terms and that, in these elementary terms, p' is tautologically equivalent to p, or is equipollent to p (see ESL, p. 108). (*I*-term).

GROUP B. REDUCTION

The procedure of reduction serves to eliminate redundant parts from a statement and to give it a form avoiding unnecessary complications. It is obvious that the definition of such a procedure is to some extent a matter of taste. However, it will be seen that the definition given leads to statement forms which appear appropriate both from general standards of taste and from the viewpoint of constructing propositional operations that appear reasonable, in particular, implications that can be interpreted as conditionals contrary to fact. However, the latter consequence will become visible only in later chapters of this presentation.

In order to carry through the reduction procedure we first define redundant parts, and then define a procedure of contraction which serves to diminish the number of binary operations in a statement. The contraction procedure is subdivided into two forms, according as the expressions referred to are synthetic or analytic. The term 'analytic' will always be used synonymously with the term 'tautological'.

Definition 3. A unit contained in a statement p is any combination of signs in p such that, if this combination is enclosed in parentheses within the statement, the resulting total expression is equisignificant to p. (*V*-term).

Definition 4. A unit is *closed* if it includes, for every argument variable occurring in it, a corresponding operator. An operator is *redundant* if its variable does not occur in any functional within its scope.

For instance, in '$(x)f(x)$' the unit '$f(x)$' is not closed, whereas the total expression is a closed unit. In '$(x)f(y)$' the operator '(x)' is redundant.

Definition 5. Double negation lines are redundant, except if their scope is a unit u_1 which is binary-connected to a unit u_2 such that u_1 is equisignificant to u_2.

The term 'binary-connected' refers to connection by means of a binary operation. The significance of the exception made in definition 5 will be explained presently. Note that the term 'scope of a negation' is meant to include the negation line. [1]

Definition 6. If u is a synthetic unit, then an elementary propositional term, or an elementary function, occurring in u is *redundant* if u can be written without this term, or function, and without replacing it by some term or function not already used in u. (V-term).

If the elementary term, or function, occurs more than once in u, the phrase 'without this term' is to mean that all occurrences of the term are eliminated. The addition about replacing the term by another one is necessary because variables can of course be given different names. For instance, in '$a.(a \mathbf{v} c)$' the term 'c' is redundant, whereas 'a' is not, although 'a' could be eliminated by replacing it by 'b', which latter term, however, does not occur in the original statement.

Definition 7. A synthetic unit u_1 is *contractible* if canceling binary-connected units within u_1 together with the sign of their connecting operations leads to a unit u_2 which is equisignificant with u_1. If and only if adding negation lines on units inside u_1 makes it possible to cancel other units, it is admitted and required for the process of contraction. The canceled units are *redundant*. (V-terms).

This definition of contraction, which applies only to binary operations, may be illustrated in application to the statement

(1) $(a \equiv b) \supset (c.d \supset a.\bar{b})$

Here u_1 is the whole formula. If the term '$a.\bar{b}$', which is binary-connected by the preceding implication sign, is canceled together with the implication sign and a negation line is added on the term

---

[1]   ESL, p. 25.

'$c.d$', the resulting form

$$(2) \qquad\qquad (a \equiv b) \supset \overline{c.d}$$

represents the unit u_2 which is equivalent to u_1. The form (2) is the reduced form of (1). Another example is given by the contraction of '$(a \supset b) \equiv b$' into '$\bar{a} \supset b$'; or in the contraction of '$a.(b \vee \bar{b})$' into 'a'. Note that in the first two examples u_2 is not a unit before the canceling, whereas it is so.in the last example.

The term 'binary-connected' makes definition 7 inapplicable to expressions like '$\overline{\bar{a}}$', within which the unit 'a' is not binary connected. The reduction of such expressions is achieved by canceling the double negation lines, which are not units, but are redundant according to definition 5.

It is possible to set up even stronger requirements for contraction; for instance, the introduction of parentheses may enable us to cancel a unit, as in the transition from '$a.b \vee a.c$' to '$a.(b \vee c)$'. But definition 7 appears sufficient for our purposes.

Whereas definitions 6–7 refer only to synthetic units, the following definition gives rules of contraction for analytic units. A separate treatment of these two cases is unavoidable, because all analytic units are equivalent to one another and therefore the condition of equisignificance does not supply a sufficient restriction for the reduction process. In fact, if the word 'reduction' is not carefully modified, every analytic statement can be 'reduced' to some such simple form as '$a \vee \bar{a}$'. Although the operation of contraction, introduced in definition 7, can be taken over for analytic units, it will therefore be modified so as to apply merely to the major operation of a unit, as follows:

Definition 8. An analytic unit u_1 whose major operation is binary is *contractible*, if canceling one major term, possibly after canceling or adding a negation line on the other major term, leads to an analytic unit u_2. The canceled term is *redundant*. (V-terms).

The following definition applies both to synthetic and analytic statements.

Definition 9. A statement, or a unit in a statement, is *reduced* if it contains no contractible units and no redundant elementary terms, functions, operators, or negation lines. (V-term).

Examples for synthetic statements:

	non-reduced form	reduced form
(3)	$(a \supset b).(a \supset \bar{b})$	$\bar{a}$
(4)	$[a \supset (\bar{c} \supset \bar{b})].[a \supset (\bar{c} \supset b)]$	$a \supset c$
(5)	$(\exists x)f(x).g(x) \lor (\exists y)f(y).\overline{g(y)}$	$(\exists x)f(x)$
(6)	$(\exists x)(\exists y)[f(x) \supset a].[f(y) \supset \bar{a}]$	$(\exists x)\overline{f(x)}$
(7)	$(x)(\exists y)(\exists z)\{f(x) \supset g(x).[h(y) \supset h(z)]\}$	$(x)[f(x) \supset g(x)]$

The application of definition 7 will here be understandable. On the left-hand side of (3), u_1 is the whole statement, and u_2 results by adding a negation line on 'a'. On the left-hand side of (4), everything is canceled following the first occurrence of the letter 'c'; then the negation line on top of this letter is canceled. This statement can also be reduced by the help of definition 6, because it contains the redundant elementary term 'b'. In (5) the redundance of an elementary function is visible only after the statement is transformed into a one-scope form (also called prenex form). This and the examples (6)–(7) show that the proof of the equivalence of the reduced form to the original form may involve tautological transformations concerning operators. In (6), for instance, the operators are moved close to their functionals, and the statement then assumes the form (3).

Double negation lines are in general redundant, according to definition 5, and thus a reduced expression carries in general no double negation lines. An exception is given by the tautology '$\bar{\bar{a}} \equiv a$', in which the double negation lines are not redundant because of the exception formulated in definition 5; this formula is therefore reduced. In contrast the formula '$\bar{\bar{a}} \lor a$' is not reduced. Although here the double negation lines are protected by the exception stated in definition 5, the formula, being synthetic, is subject to contraction according to definition 7 and can be reduced to 'a'. Similarly '$\bar{\bar{a}} \supset a$' is reduced, whereas '$\bar{\bar{a}}.a$' can be contracted into 'a'. It follows that an expression of the form '$\bar{\bar{a}}$' can keep its double negation lines only if it is a major term in a binary tautological unit.

A conjunction of a synthetic statement and a tautology is not reduced, because the tautology can be canceled according to definition 7. A conjunction of tautologies is not reduced, either, because definition 8 applies. This definition also rules out forms like '$a.\bar{a} \supset b$' and '$a \supset b \vee \bar{b}$', which represent unreasonable implications. Note that these forms are also ruled out if they occur as units within a more comprehensive expression which is analytic, since the term 'major operation' in definition 8 refers only to the unit considered. However, the contraction defined in definition 8 differs from the contraction defined in definition 7 inasmuch as definition 8 requires that the unit u_2 be identical with a major term, or the negation of a major term, of u_1. Furthermore, because a tautology includes synthetic units, definitions 6–7 can be applied to its inner structure, and it can contain contractible synthetic units or, within a synthetic unit, redundant elementary terms or functions. Finally, a tautology can have redundant operators. The reduction process for tautologies requires that all these redundant parts be eliminated.

Examples for tautologies:

	non-reduced form	reduced form
(8)	$a.b.(a \vee c) \supset a$	$a.b \supset a$
(9)	$(x)(\exists y)[\overline{\overline{f(x)}} \vee \overline{f(x)}]$	$(x)[f(x) \vee \overline{f(x)}]$
(10)	$(\exists x)f(x) \vee (\exists x)(\exists y)[f(x) \supset a].[f(y) \supset \bar{a}]$	$(\exists x)f(x) \vee (\exists x)\overline{f(x)}$

Note that the form on the right in (8) is not contractible, although 'b' can be canceled while the statement remains tautologically equivalent. But this kind of contraction applies only to synthetic units, according to definition 7, while definition 8 cannot be used here. For the treatment of (10) we refer to (6).

Since in the contraction process, according to definitions 7 and 8, the number of binary operations becomes smaller, a repeated application of the process cannot lead back to the original unit and must come to an end. Likewise, canceling of double negation lines cannot lead back to the original formula. These results guarantee that for every statement there exists a reduced form. Furthermore, it is easily seen that, if a synthetic statement contains an analytic, or a contradictory, unit, this unit can always be eliminated by the use of the operations described in definition 7. Since double negation lines, as was mentioned, are exempt from the cancelation process only if they stand over a major term of a tautological unit, it follows that a reduced synthetic statement cannot contain double negation lines; such lines can remain only within tautologies. Moreover, no reduced statement, whether analytic or synthetic, can contain a contractible unit (definition 7 or 8), because the reduction process would eliminate such units. We thus arrive at the theorem:

Theorem 1. For every statement, there exists at least one reduced form. In a reduced synthetic statement, every unit is reduced; this applies likewise to reduced analytic statements except for possible double negation lines on certain units.

An example of a reduced analytic statement containing a non-reduced synthetic unit is given by the statement '$\overline{\overline{a}} \supset a$', where the synthetic unit '$\overline{a}$', taken separately, is not reduced. In synthetic statements, such nonreduced units cannot occur.

GROUP C. NORMAL FORMS

Assume a synthetic statement p is written in a reduced and closed one-scope form with a minimum of argument variables. The argument variables are thus all assumed to be bound; i.e., special constant values of these variables do not occur. Each elementary functional may be regarded as a propositional variable 'e_1', 'e_2', ..., in such a way that different propositional variables are used even for different functionals of the same function if they differ in the argument variables, such as '$f(x)$' and '$f(y)$'. We now cancel the operators; the resulting formula is called the *matrix* of p.

If a statement p in the lower functional calculus is given in any form, it is always possible to write it in a one-scope form, according to a familiar theorem. Although the rule of using a minimum number of argument variables restricts the possible forms of matrices thus resulting for a statement, there may exist several matrices for it which are not propositionally equivalent. For instance, when p is given as a conjunction of two statements each of which has two major all-operators, these two statements can be merged into a one-scope form by identifying the variables governed by all-operators; but this identification can be done in two ways, and thus different matrices may result.

By making derivations in the calculus of propositions from the matrix of p, if this statement is given in a certain reduced one-scope form, we arrive at statements q which are *propositionally derivable* from p. For instance, the statement

(11) $\qquad\qquad (x)(y)[\overline{f(x)} \supset g(x, y)]$

is propositionally derivable from

(12) $\qquad\qquad (x)(y)[\overline{f(x)} \vee h(x) \supset f(y) . g(x, y)]$

whereas the formula

(13) $\qquad\qquad\qquad (x)f(x)$

though derivable from (12), is not propositionally derivable from it. We will say that (13) is *operator-derivable* from (12). If q is propositionally derivable from p, the implication from the matrix of p to the matrix of q is a tautology in the calculus of propositions.

Since (13) is derivable from (12), we can add it conjunctively to (12); and we can also add it in a form in which the variable 'x' is replaced by 'y'. Merging the two scopes, we arrive at the form

(14) $\qquad (x)(y)\{[\overline{f(x)} \vee h(x) \supset f(y) . g(x, y)] . f(x) . f(y)\}$

This form is tautologically equivalent with (12). But the operand of (14) is not tautologically equivalent with the operand of (12). Furthermore, whereas (12) is reduced, (14) is not reduced, because we can cancel the factors '$f(x)$' and '$f(y)$' while keeping the statement tautologically equivalent.

It is possible to make further derivations in terms of operator rules and thus to construct further operator-derivable statements. We can interchange the variables 'x' and 'y' in (12) and add the result to (14); and we can make the variables 'x' and 'y' identical. Thus (14) assumes the form:

(15)
$$(x)(y)\{[\overline{f(x)} \vee h(x) \supset f(y) . g(x, y)] . [\overline{f(y)} \vee h(y) \supset f(x) . g(y, x)]$$
$$. [\overline{f(x)} \vee h(x) \supset f(x) . g(x, x)] . [\overline{f(y)} \vee h(y) \supset f(y) . g(y, y)]\}$$

Here we have omitted the factors '$f(x)$' and '$f(y)$' of (14), because they are now propositionally derivable from the operand of (15). The form (15) contains several elementary terms not contained in (12), such as '$g(y, x)$', '$h(y)$', etc. Note that (15) is not reduced, because it is equivalent to the shorter form (12).

When we restrict derivations by the condition that the operator set of (12) must not be changed although some of the operators may become redundant, that the number of argument variables must not be increased, and that no elementary terms must be introduced other than resulting from the functions contained in (12) by inserting the argument variables in different ways [1], no further addition to (15) can be made, except for terms which are propositionally derivable from the operand of (15). Regarding the functionals of (15) as separate elementary terms 'e_1' ... 'e_n', we shall call the operand of (15) the *complete matrix* of (12). From it all the expressions subject to the restrictions mentioned are propositionally derivable; and with respect to these expressions, the complete matrix is the full propositional equivalent of the original statement.

For the definition of the complete matrix we shall add the requirement that it be constructed from a one-scope form which has a minimum number of variables. This requirement is satisfied by (12). It was mentioned above that the minimum requirement does not uniquely determine the matrix. Now it is easily seen that for minimum forms which have the same operator set, or can be made to have the same set by suitable naming of variables and arranging the order of commutative operators, the complete matrix is the same. The reason is that these forms lead to identical classes of derivable statements possessing the same operator set as the original form, or a subset of it. Therefore, if the operator set of the minimum one-scope form is given, the complete matrix is determined.

The question arises: if two minimum one-scope forms of the same synthetic statement are given, must they possess the same

---

[1] Note that this condition also excludes the substitution of special constant values for the variables.

operator set? The latter term is to mean that the operator sets can be made identical by suitable naming of variables and interchanging of commutative operators. I do not know of a proof answering this question in the affirmative, and I do not know any instance to the contrary. I think this is a problem that should attract the attention of the logicians. Until it is solved, I shall proceed on the assumption that there are different minimum operator sets, and thus also different complete matrices, for a given synthetic statement. If it should be possible to prove the contrary, the application of the present theory will be simplified, but the theory will not be invalidated.

Since there is only a finite number of possible operator sets for a minimum one-scope form, the class of complete matrices is finite and constitutes a characteristic for a given synthetic statement. It may sometimes be difficult to find the complete matrices; and we have no general method to prove that a certain form represents such a matrix. This question is closely connected with the decision problem, for which even in the simple calculus of functions no general solution exists. But for statements of a none too complicated form the class of complete matrices can be found; and it is often possible to prove that there is only one complete matrix, as for the example (12). We only have to go through the various other possible forms of operator sets in two variables and to show that such operator sets do not furnish equivalent one-scope forms. The present theory is restricted to formulae for which the class of complete matrices can be determined; this is a permissible restriction, because laws of nature and 'reasonable' operations will always be represented in rather simple formulae.

Using a supplemented matrix of a statement, we can expand it disjunctively in elementary T-cases (ESL, p. 52, p. 361), or conjunctively in negated F-cases. We now define:

Definition 10. By a *D-form* of a synthetic statement we understand the formula resulting when the elementary terms of a complete matrix of the statement are written as a disjunctive expansion in elementary T-cases and the original operator set is put before the expansion. By a *C-form* of a synthetic statement we understand the formula resulting when the complete matrix of the statement is conjunctively expanded in negated elementary F-cases. (V-terms).

Although 'D-form' and 'C-form' are V-terms, referring to a mode of writing a statement, it is an I-property of a synthetic statement to have a certain class of D-forms, or C-forms. If the synthetic statement contains no variables, or only propositional variables, the forms are also defined; they then contain no operators.

If the elementary terms of the complete matrix are abbreviated by 'e_1' ... 'e_n', all 2^n possible combinations of these terms can be written as follows:

$$(16) \quad (\ ) \dots (\ )[(e_1 \dots \ e_n) \vee (e_1 \dots \ \bar{e}_n) \vee \dots \vee (\bar{e}_1 \dots \ \bar{e}_n)]$$

$$(17) \quad (\ ) \dots (\ )[(e_1 \vee \dots \vee e_n) . (e_1 \vee \dots \vee \bar{e}_n) \dots (\bar{e}_1 \vee \dots \vee \bar{e}_n)]$$

The D-form results from (16) by omitting certain terms of the disjunction. The C-form results from (17) by omitting certain factors of the conjunction. The variables 'x', 'y', etc., are contained in the terms abbreviated by 'e_1' ... 'e_n'. The D-form results from the C-form by 'multiplying out', and vice versa. Furthermore, the D-form can be constructed from the C-form as follows: we take the conjunction of the omitted factors of (17) and negate it; breaking this long negation line until we arrive at the shortest negation lines, we find the D-form. This follows because the omitted factors of (17) are the negated T-cases of the statement.

If we restrict disjunctive and conjunctive normal forms to a given set of elementary terms and add the condition that no mere duplications of terms or factors are admitted, a D-form is the longest version of a disjunctive normal form, and a C-form is the longest version of a conjunctive normal form. Shorter versions result by merging terms, or factors; as for instance by using the equivalences

$$(18) \qquad\qquad e_1 . e_2 . e_3 \vee e_1 . e_2 . \bar{e}_3 \equiv e_1 . e_2$$

$$(19) \qquad\qquad (e_1 \vee e_2 \vee e_3) . (e_1 \vee e_2 \vee \bar{e}_3) \equiv e_1 \vee e_2$$

Definition 11. If a tautology is given in one-scope form, we construct its D-form by expanding its matrix in elementary

T-cases, using those elementary terms which occur in the given statement. (V-term).

The D-form of a tautology is the complete expansion (16). Note that a tautology has no C-form, because it has no F-cases. The complete expansion (17) is a contradiction.

Definition 12. When we add certain elementary terms to those contained in the complete matrix and then construct expansions in elementary terms equivalent to D-form or C-form, we obtain an *elongated D-form*, or *elongated C-form*. (V-term).

For instance, if '$a \equiv b$' is given, its D-form is

$$(20) \qquad\qquad a.b \lor \bar{a}.\bar{b}$$

An elongated D-form is

$$(21) \qquad\qquad a.b.c \lor a.b.\bar{c} \lor \bar{a}.\bar{b}.c \lor \bar{a}.\bar{b}.\bar{c}$$

Group D. All-statements

Definition 13. A synthetic statement p is an *all-statement* if and only if the operator set of its D-form (or C-form) contains at least one all-operator. (I-term).

Definition 14. A statement is *written as an all-statement* if and only if it is written with a non-redundant all-operator whose scope is the whole statement. (V-term).

Note that definition 14 can be applied to tautologies, whereas definition 13 cannot be so applied.

Group E. Residuals

Residuals are definable for all forms of statements. They are used to characterize certain properties of the statement, in particular, *exhaustiveness*, which term applies when all the possibilities opened up by a statement are exhausted by the objects of the physical world. A non-exhaustive statement includes empty parts. This property is of special importance for all-statements, but is also defined for other statements. Furthermore, residuals will be used to define a kind of generality that refers to all-statements only.

Definition 15. A *disjunctive residual in elementary terms* of a statement p is any statement resulting when p is written in D-form and one or several terms of the operand are canceled. (I-term if p is synthetic, V-term if p is analytic.)

Definition 16. A statement p which is verifiably true is *exhaustive in elementary terms* if none of its disjunctive residuals in elementary terms, for any of its D-forms, is verifiably true. (I-term if p is synthetic, V-term if p is analytic.)

For instance, the statement

$$(22a) \qquad\qquad (x)[f(x).g(x) \equiv h(x)]$$

has the following D-form:

$$(22b) \quad (x)[f(x).g(x).h(x) \mathbf{v} f(x).\overline{g(x)}.\overline{h(x)} \mathbf{v} \overline{f(x)}.g(x).\overline{h(x)} \mathbf{v} \overline{f(x)}.\overline{g(x)}.h(x)]$$

The statement (22a) is not exhaustive in elementary terms if canceling any one, or any two, or any three, of the four terms in the brackets of (22b) leads to a statement which is verifiably true. If a tautology contains only variables, it is always exhaustive in elementary terms.

Definition 17. A *disjunctive residual in major terms* of p is any statement resulting when p is expanded in a disjunction of major T-cases (ESL, p. 52, p. 362) and one or several terms of the operand are canceled. (V-term).

Definition 18. A statement p which is verifiably true is *exhaustive in major terms* if none of its disjunctive residuals in major terms is verifiably true. (V-term).

Note that a conjunction as well as a statement whose major operation is a negation, if they are verifiably true, are always exhaustive in major terms, because they have no disjunctive residuals in major terms.

Definition 19. A statement p_1 which is verifiably true is *exhaustive except for p* (in major or elementary terms), if all its verifiably true disjunctive residuals in major or elementary terms, if there are any, are derivable from p. (I-term for elementary terms, V-term for major terms.)

The use of this definition will be seen in the discussion of definition 35. Note that if p_1 is exhaustive, it is also exhaustive except for p, for any p. It can happen that a major disjunctive residual of p_1 is derivable from p_1 while p_1 is exhaustive in elementary terms; then

p_1 is exhaustive in major terms *except for itself* (see the discussion of (43)).

Definition 20. A *conjunctive residual* of a synthetic statement p is any statement resulting when p is written in C-form and one or several factors of the operand are canceled. (I-term).

Definition 21. A disjunctive, or conjunctive, *extension* of a statement results from its D-form, or its C-form, by adding terms, or factors, from the total expansion (16) or (17). (V-term).

Obviously, canceling terms in the D-form is the same as adding factors to the C-form, and vice-versa. Therefore, a disjunctive residual is tautologically equivalent to a conjunctive extension, and a conjunctive residual is tautologically equivalent to a disjunctive extension. Note that an analytic statement has no conjunctive residuals because it has no C-form.

Using conjunctive extensions, we can find out whether a given expansion is exhaustive in elementary terms. For instance, if we expand the matrix of (12) in elementary T-cases, we can prove that it is not exhaustive, because the conjunctive extension (14) is true. This shows that it is important to construct the D-form from the complete matrix. Otherwise many statements would not be exhaustive in elementary terms, because a conjunctive extension, or a disjunctive residual, would be derivable from the statement itself. The definition of exhaustiveness in terms of the complete matrix excludes this possibility.

From familiar properties of conjunctive normal forms we derive the following theorem:

Theorem 2. If a synthetic statement q is derivable from a synthetic statement p, while the operator set of q is a subset of that of p, both referred to C-forms, and the elementary terms of q are contained among those of p, then q can be written as a conjunctive residual of p, and p can be written as a disjunctive residual of q, or of an elongated D-form of q.

Definition 22. If the C-form of p is tautologically equivalent to a conjunction of two of its residuals, each of these residuals is called *self-contained* within p. (I-term).

With the help of theorem 1 we derive:

Theorem 3. If p contains a closed unit which is derivable

from p, then this unit is tautologically equivalent to a self-contained conjunctive residual of p.

Definition 23. A statement p is *general in self-contained factors* if, for any of its C-forms, each of its self-contained conjunctive residuals, after being reduced, possesses at least one non-redundant all-operator. (I-term).

For instance, the statement

$$(23) \qquad (x)(\mathcal{Z}y)\{[f(x) \supset g(x)].h(y)\}$$

is not general in self-contained factors, because it can be written as the conjunction of its two residuals

$$(24) \qquad (x)[f(x) \supset g(x)].(\mathcal{Z}y)h(y)$$

the second of which possesses no all-operator. However, (23) would be general in self-contained factors if the second operator were an all-operator, or if '$h(y)$' were replaced by '$h(x, y)$'.

Combining theorem 3 and definition 23, we derive:

Theorem 4. If a synthetic statement p, which is general in self-contained factors, can be written in a reduced form containing a closed unit q that is derivable from p, then q is an all-statement.

This theorem shows that definition 23 formulates a property which ensures generality for closed units within a statement.

GROUP F. UNIVERSAL STATEMENTS

Definition 24. An *individual-term* is a term which is defined with reference to a certain space-time region, or which can be so defined without change of meaning. (I-term).

The term can be a proper name or a definite description. The addition refers to languages in which terms like 'terrestrial' are used as primitive terms. If the language is rich enough to possess space-time coordinates, it can be shown that the meaning of the term can be equivalently defined by reference to the space-time region 'Earth'. Languages which do not possess the means to formulate space-time coordinates are disregarded in the theory of nomological operations, which are intended to account for the language of science. The phrase 'can be defined' refers to logical possibility, and therefore presupposes only the definition of tautologies, or logical formulae, but does not presuppose synthetic nomological statements.

Definition 25. A synthetic statement is *universal* if it cannot be written in a reduced form which contains an individual-term. (*I*-term).

Definition 25a. A statement is *written as a universal statement* if it contains no individual-term. (*V*-term).

Note that definition 25a can be applied to tautologies, whereas definition 25 cannot be so applied.

Since the units of measure are usually defined with reference to an individual standard, such as the meter standard preserved in Paris, the numerical values of physical constants are excluded by definition 25 from the content of physical laws. But this consequence appears reasonable because these constants merely express relationships to the standard. That the speed of light is 3.10^{10} centimeters per second is a relation between light, the meter standard in Paris, and the revolving earth. The physical law states merely that the speed of light is a constant. It is different when standards are defined through class terms, for instance, when the unit of length is defined by the wave length of the cadmium line. Measured in such standards, the numerical values of physical constants belong to the content of the law.

The omission of universal values defined with reference to individuals does not represent any disadvantage for our conception of laws of nature. For all scientific as well as practical applications, the numerical value of a quantity has only an intermediate use: it serves for computing relationships between this quantity and others. For instance, the numerical values in the decimal system may serve to compute the ratio between the speed of light and the speed of sound. We can imagine the system of knowledge as given in the form of the totality of laws of nature, supplemented by a table of numerical constants. This table is indispensable for practical applications, but does not belong in the nomological part of knowledge.

Furthermore, definition 25 excludes the use of definitions of class terms by reference to samples. For instance, copper might be defined as anything that is like a certain sample in certain respects, say, that has the same atomic weight as the sample. Such definitions are not used in the formulation of scientific laws. This is illustrated by the discovery of isotopes; if the given definition of a substance were used, there could not be any forms of the substance having a different atomic weight. If interpreted in the sense of this and the preceding qualification, the usual laws of nature cannot be written in a reduced form which contains an individual-term. [1]

A certain ambiguity arises because a natural language is often capable of different rational reconstructions. The term 'polar bear', for instance, can be interpreted as meaning a bear living in the polar regions of the Earth, in which interpretation it would be an individual-term. It could also be defined as a biological species of certain general characteristics, for instance, as a bear with a white skin, etc. In such cases, we have two rational reconstructions which are not logically equivalent, though perhaps practically equivalent. As a consequence, a statement which in one rational reconstruction is nomological, may not be so in another reconstruction of conversational language. This ambiguity, however, offers no difficulties, since the class of nomological statements is defined only for a certain reconstruction of language. If a statement of conversational language is given, it would be meaningless to ask: is this statement really nomological? There is no such thing as an absolute meaning of the terms of a natural language. A classification of statements such as expressed in categories like 'analytic' or 'nomological' refers to a given rational reconstruction of language. Whether this reconstruction is adequate, is to be investigated separately.

In other words, when we say that a statement like 'copper has an atomic weight of 63.5' is a law of nature, this should be understood as meaning, 'there exists an adequate rational reconstruction of language in which this statement is a law of nature'. That there may also exist a rational reconstruction in which copper is defined by reference to an individual sample and for which the statement

---

[1] I think this answers N. Goodman's remark that, if my definition of universal statement is used, 'virtually all apparently universal sentences will be ruled out'. (l.c.p. 101).

is not a law of nature, is irrelevant. In fact, the second reconstruction may appear less adequate for the very reason that it does not account for the usage of calling the statement considered a law of nature. If a language is to be rationally reconstructed, it is advisable not merely to look for definitions that coincide extensionally with usage of terms, but also to adjust definitions to the usage of such categories as 'law of nature', 'analytic', etc. Only the total reconstruction, as a whole, can be judged as adequate. For instance, defining 'human being' as 'featherless biped' would correspond extensionally to usage; but it would contradict such statements as 'featherless bipeds are not necessarily human beings', which we also find among linguistic usage.

It may even be possible to construct a definition of original nomological statements which allows for the occurrence of certain individual-terms; for such a reconstruction it would be possible also to admit, in such statements, terms defined by reference to samples, etc. Interpretations of this kind may be as adequate as the one presented here. All the present investigation is intended to achieve is one adequate reconstruction of the term 'law of nature', without claiming that this is the only one.

The addition concerning a reduced form, given in definition 25, is necessary because otherwise we could insert into any statement redundant individual-terms, for instance, by adding a tautology containing an individual term. The phrase 'cannot be written' excludes hidden individual-terms. For instance, we could define an individual by the use of class terms alone (ESL, p. 257) and eliminate the iota-operator; the resulting statement would not directly contain an individual-term. This is excluded because the resulting statement could be transformed so as to contain an iota-operator. An example for an excluded statement is given by 'for all x, if x is a man that has seen a living human retina, and no other person has seen such a retina before x, then x contributed to the establishment of the principle of the conservation of energy'. This sentence, which is true, contains in a hidden form a description of H. v. Helmholtz, and is therefore not universal.

A further condition must now be added. If an individual-term is introduced by means of a definite description, it is possible to eliminate the iota-operator and then to derive a statement which is no longer tautologically equivalent to the original statement. Since this statement is not tautologically transformable into a statement containing an iota-operator, it is universal in the sense of definition 25; but it still includes a reference to an individual in a hidden form and does not possess the kind of generality which is to be required for a law of nature. [1]

Consider the statement, 'all stars which H. v. Helmholtz saw were at least of the 11-th magnitude [2]'. This statement cannot be regarded as a law of nature, because it merely expresses the technical limitations of telescopes available at the time when Helmholtz lived. In the form given, it is ruled out as not being universal, according to definition 25. However, replacing the term 'H. v. Helmholtz' by the definite description mentioned, we can now derive the statement, 'all stars seen by any man who saw a living human retina before any other man saw one, were at least of the 11-th magnitude'. The latter statement does not express the fact that there was such a man, and it thus cannot be transformed back into the form containing an iota-operator. This statement, therefore, is universal in the sense of definition 25.

In order to rule out statements of this kind, we shall add a further condition to the requirement of exhaustiveness, introduced in definitions 16 and 18. The statement contains a function '$\hat{x}$ saw a living human retina before any other man saw one', which may be abbreviated by '$sr(\hat{x})$'. This function is satisfied by one and only one argument x, which existed only during a restricted space-time region r; we therefore have the relation, which is verifiably true,

(24a) $(x)[sr(x) \supset r(x)]$

Let us now write the statement under consideration in the following

---

[1]   I am indebted to C. Hempel and D. Kalish for having drawn my attention to this problem.

[2]   The term '11-th magnitude' contains, in its usual definition, a reference to the earth and thus would represent an individual-term. But it could be replaced by a term expressing light intensity at the point of observation, using a measure not depending on the earth as a reference point, for instance photons per unit of time.

form, using 'st' for 'star', 's' for 'see', and 'm' for 'at least of 11-th magnitude':

(24b) $$(x)(y)[st(y).s(x, y).sr(x) \supset m(y)]$$

We will abbreviate the implicans by '$g(x,y)$' and expand the statement in major T-cases, with the modification, however, that the term '$r(x)$' is added:

(24c) $$(x)(y)[r(x) \vee g(x, y).m(y) \vee \overline{g(x, y)}.m(y) \vee \overline{g(x, y)}.\overline{m(y)}]$$

The term '$g(x, y).m(y)$' can here be canceled, since this term implies '$r(x)$' according to (24a). This follows because '$(a \vee b).(b \supset a)$' is equivalent to 'a'. Note that this derivation would also be possible if the operators in (24c) were existential operators, if only the operator in (24a) is an all-operator. Calling (24c) an *r-expansion* of (24b), we thus find that a disjunctive residual of the *r*-expansion is verifiably true; i.e., that the *r*-expansion is not exhaustive. We understand here by a residual, as above, a form resulting when a term stemming from the original statement is canceled; canceling of '$r(x)$' is not regarded as constituting a residual, since such canceling is always possible.

The fact that statement (24b) contains an unreasonable function, namely '$sr(\hat{x})$', whose extension is restricted to a certain space-time region r, thus finds its expression in the result that the statement is not exhaustive in its *r*-expansion. This criterion, which can likewise be applied to an expression in D-form, enables us to rule out statements which are non-equivalently derived from statements containing individual-terms. Note that we thus also rule out functions whose extension contains more than one individual, if only the extension is verifiably restricted to a certain space-time region. We now define:

Definition 26. A statement p is *unrestrictedly exhaustive*, in major or elementary terms, if there exists no restricted space-time region r, for any of its variables, such that the *r*-expansion of p is not exhaustive.

By a restricted space-time region we understand an undivided part of the universe, which however is not identical with the universe. Such a region might be given by a part of the earth's surface during a certain time, or by a galaxy. The condition of being unrestrictedly exhaustive rules out all-statements which are verified by examining all individuals of a certain kind within such a region. It amounts to requiring that the statement be exhaustive even if any region r is excluded from the range of its all-operator. Note that a statement which is unrestrictedly exhaustive is also exhaustive.

The question may be posed whether the condition of being unrestrictedly exhaustive can be used to replace the condition that the statement should contain no individual-terms. The answer is negative; both conditions are needed. The example concerning stars up to the 11th magnitude has shown that the condition of being unrestrictedly exhaustive cannot be dispensed with. The following example shows that the other condition is also indispensable. Assume that Peter weighs as much as Paul. The statement, 'for all x, if and only if x weighs as much as Peter, x weighs as much as Paul', is then true; and it is unrestrictedly exhaustive. But it cannot be regarded as a law of nature; it represents merely a complicated way of saying that Peter weighs as much as Paul. [1] In order to rule out this statement from nomological statements, we need the condition that the use of individual-terms is not admitted for original nomological statements, a condition which this statement violates.

With the exclusion of individual-terms, the theory developed is greatly simplified from a formal point of view. Within the chapter on original nomological statements, the argument variables 'x', 'y', etc., can always be assumed to be either bound variables, or free variables with respect to the whole statement, i.e., variables for which any value may be substituted. Since such variables can always be bound, the theory of original nomological statements can, in principle, be restricted to bound argument variables. The

---

[1] Note, however, that the transitivity, symmetry, and reflexivity of the relation 'weighs as much as' must be regarded, not as analytic, but as verified by experience, when 'weighing as much as' is defined by a scale being in balance. Since these properties are presupposed for deriving the equivalence of the two statements, this equivalence is not analytic.

use of free variables, however, is sometimes advisable for reasons of convenience.

Consequently, we need not consider in this chapter derivations consisting in the substitution of special values for argument variables, as for instance, the transition form '$(x)f(x)$' to '$f(x_1)$', where 'x_1' refers to some specified individual. It is for this reason that the concept of a complete matrix, introduced in group C, is sufficient to cover all possible derivations considered. Even for derivative nomological statements, where individual-terms will be admitted, it follows that such terms always occupy places which could also be occupied by free variables.

III

ORIGINAL NOMOLOGICAL STATEMENTS

We now possess the notational means to lay down the requirements defining original nomological statements. Under I-requirement we classify those requirements which, for synthetic statements, formulate invariant properties, though most of these requirements, with the only exception of 1.1, formulate variant properties for tautologies. It is therefore understood that, if p is analytic, the requirements refer only to the form of p as it is written. For instance, requirement 1.3, then means that p must be written as an all-statement. Requirement 1.5 drops out for analytic statements.

I-Requirements for original nomological statements

Requirement 1.1.   The statement p must be verifiably true. (Definition 1).

Requirement 1.2.   The statement p must be universal. (Definitions 24, 25, 25a).

Requirement 1.3.   The statement p must be an all-statement. (Definitions 13–14).

Requirement 1.4.   The statement p must be unrestrictedly exhaustive in elementary terms. (Definition 26).

Requirement 1.5.   If the statement p is synthetic, it must be general in self-contained factors. (Definition 23).

Of these requirements, only 1.5 was not used in my earlier presentation. I will therefore explain the significance of this requirement. In combination with the other requirements, it serves to ensure, for original nomological statements of the synthetic kind, generality in a reasonable sense; in fact, 1.1–1.5 may be regarded as requirements defining a *proper all-statement*. For analytic statements, generality in self-contained factors is not defined, but no requirement of this kind appears here necessary because analytic statements are always general.

Not always is lack of generality an indication of non-nomological character. There are *purely existential* statements, i.e., statements which in D-form or C-form possess only existential operators, which we would not hesitate to recognize as laws of nature. In the theory here presented, such statements are constructed by a derivation from original nomological statements and are therefore, in a terminology to be explained in definition 28, nomological. Consider, for instance, the statement, 'all things contain elementary particles'. This is true even for elementary particles, if 'contain' is regarded as a reflexive relation, such that a particle contains itself. The statement can be written, with 'ep' for 'elementary particle' and 'c' for 'contains', in the form

$$(25) \qquad (x)(\exists y)ep(y).c(x, y)$$

This is an original nomological statement, since it satisfies all the requirements 1.1–1.9. It contains the purely existential conjunctive residual

$$(26) \qquad (\exists y)ep(y)$$

But this is not a self-contained residual of (25), because its variable 'y' also occurs in the other functional of (25); thus (25) is not tautologically equivalent to the conjunction

$$(27) \qquad (\exists y)ep(y).(x)(\exists y)c(x, y)$$

Therefore requirement 1.5 is not violated, and (25) is general in self-contained factors.

Now since we can derive from (25) the statement (26), this purely existential statement, reading, 'there are elementary particles', is nomological. But it appears reasonable to regard this statement as a law of nature, because it is indispensable to the formulation of the law that all things contain elementary particles. This illustration shows why we restricted, in requirement 1.5, the non-redundance of an all-operator to self-contained residuals. If a variable governed by an existential operator occurs in two functionals connected by an 'and', this conjunction states more than a conjunction of

existential statements with different variables, such as given in
(27). A non-self-contained existential residual may therefore be
tolerated in original nomological statements and becomes, in turn,
nomological.

In contrast to the statement 'there are elementary particles',
a statement like 'there is copper' is much more specific; and we
would consider this statement as referring merely to a matter of
fact, thus refusing to regard it as nomological. It appears therefore
satisfactory that in the present theory this statement is not nomological because it cannot be derived from original nomological
statements.

The following consideration may make these relations clear. We
might try to make the statement about the existence of copper
nomological by inserting it in an original nomological statement.
For instance, we might use the form (23), with 'h' for 'copper',
while the first part of (23) might be the reasonable implication,
'if a metal is heated (f), it expands (g)'. In this interpretation, (23)
satisfies all the requirements 1.1–1.4. But it does not satisfy
requirement 1.5, because it possesses the self-contained conjunctive
residual '$(\exists y)h(y)$'. Therefore we cannot in this way take the
statement about the existence of copper nomological.

This result, however, is not yet satisfactory. It only shows that,
if p is original-nomological, it cannot contain a purely existential
closed unit which is derivable from p (theorem 4). However, there
are other forms of statements p, which contain a closed existential
unit in such a way that this unit is not derivable from p, whereas p
appears unreasonable nonetheless. Consider the statement

(28) $(x)\{f(x) \supset [g(x).(\exists y)h(y)]\}$

From it we can derive the all-statement

(29) $(x)[f(x) \supset (\exists y)h(y)]$

Though here the purely existential closed unit '$(\exists y)h(y)$' is not
derivable, the derivable statement (29) appears unreasonable, as is
easily seen if the above interpretations f = heated metal, g = expands, h = copper, are used.

It will now be shown that this kind of statement is ruled out by requirement 1.4. This is achieved by the following theorem:

Theorem 5. If a statement p can be written in a form which is reduced and contains a closed unit q, then either q, or $\bar{q}$, is derivable from p, or p is not exhaustive in elementary terms.

The significance of this theorem for synthetic statements p and q is as follows. If q is derivable from p and p satisfies requirement 1.5, we know from theorem 4 that q is an all-statement; therefore q does not present an existential statement of the merely factual kind, like 'there exists copper', which cannot be regarded as a law of nature. If $\bar{q}$ is derivable, we know that q is false, and thus q is no longer dangerous. In this case, requirement 1.5 guarantees that $\bar{q}$ satisfies the conditions appropriate for a law of nature; its negation q is not subject to such conditions. The negation of a nomological statement is not bound to structural requirements; for instance, the negation of a proper all-statement is a merely factual existential statement. If neither q nor $\bar{q}$ is derivable from p, theorem 5 says that the statement p is not exhaustive in elementary terms and therefore not original-nomological. An example for the latter case is given by (28) where q is '$(\exists y)h(y)$'.

If q is analytic, it is derivable from every p, and therefore theorem 5 is satisfied. If p is analytic and q is synthetic, q is not derivable from p; but in this case the following proof of nonexhaustiveness remains valid. For these reasons, theorem 5 is not restricted to synthetic statements, but applies likewise to analytic statements. It is true that, if q is analytic, we cannot use theorem 4. However, according to a remark above (following the formulation of requirement 1.5), analytic statements are always general and do not need a specific requirement concerning generality.

The proof of theorem 5 is somewhat complicated, because exhaustiveness in elementary terms refers to a one-scope form of p. If q includes bound variables (and this is the very case which interests us), its operators will thus be separated from its operand, and the D-form of p will include indefinite expressions stemming from q, like '$h(y)$', which are capable of different truth values.

To prove theorem 5, we first write p in a reduced form which contains the definite unit q. Now q is treated as an elementary term, and the statement p is written like a D-form with the difference that the definite unit q is not decomposed, but figures as one among the elementary terms. We call this form the *q-expansion of p*. It is written with a minimum number of argument variables, among which, however, the variables of q are not contained. This form can be written

$$(30) \qquad ( )\ldots( )[(s_1 \vee \ldots \vee s_n).q \vee (t_1 \vee \ldots \vee t_m).\bar{q}]$$

where the terms s_i and t_k are conjunctions of the elementary terms of p, but do not contain q or those elementary terms which occur exclusively inside q.

Since q is closed, it is either true or false, and thus one of the two terms inside the brackets of (30) can be canceled. In other words, the q-expansion of p is not exhaustive, one of its residuals being true. Exception is to be made for the case that either no q-terms, or no $\bar{q}$-terms, occur in (30). But then $\bar{q}$, or q, is derivable from p, and thus theorem 5 is satisfied. We therefore proceed on the assumption that this case does not occur.

We now shall prove that the non-exhaustiveness of the q-expansion (30) is transferred to the D-form of p. This proof is somewhat complicated by the following consideration. Some of the s_i and the t_k may be identical; let us say that r such terms are identical, and let us write these r terms as the last $n{-}r$, or $m{-}r$, terms, respectively. Then (30) assumes the form

$$(31) \quad ( )\ldots( )[(s_1 \vee \ldots \vee s_{n-r}).q \vee (t_1 \vee \ldots \vee t_{m-r}).\bar{q} \vee (s_{n-r+1} \vee \ldots \vee s_n).(q \vee \bar{q})]$$

The tautology $q \vee \bar{q}$ in the third term can be canceled; but apart from special cases to be discussed presently, (31) will then no longer be a q-expansion. Furthermore, one, or two, of the three terms of (31) may vanish, i.e., need not occur in the expansion. Let us begin by studying these simpler cases; after this discussion we shall examine the general case.

If two terms vanish and one of them is the last term, there remains either the q-term, or the $\bar{q}$-term. Then q, or $\bar{q}$, is derivable from p, which case was already excluded as satisfying theorem 5. If the first two terms vanish, we can cancel in the remaining third term the tautology $q \vee \bar{q}$. This shows that p can be written without the unit q. Then q is redundant and p is not reduced. This case was excluded in theorem 5. It follows that we have to consider only cases where one term vanishes.

Let us first assume that the third term vanishes. We then have $r = 0$, and (31) assumes the form (30). In order to transform (30) into a D-form of p, we write q in D-form and then move the operators of q to the front of the whole expression. Those variables of q which are bound by all-operators must thereby be given different names in q and $\bar{q}$, because of the disjunctive form of the brackets in (30); those variables of q which are bound by existential operators are given the same names in q and $\bar{q}$. But all these variables have names different from those of the variables occurring in the s_i and t_k, because the latter variables are already bound by operators. When we denote the operands of q and $\bar{q}$ by 'q_1' and 'q_2', respectively, we thus arrive at the form

(32) $\qquad ( )...( )[(s_1 \vee ... \vee s_n).q_1 \vee (t_1 \vee ... \vee t_m).q_2]$

This form is not exhaustive for the same reasons as explained for (30); one term in the brackets of (32) can be canceled, since the remaining statement is tautologically equivalent with the corresponding remaining statement of (30). But this result is not sufficient for our purpose. It is possible that the number of argument variables stemming from q in (32) can be reduced to a smaller number; then (32) is not a D-form. We therefore must prove that the statement remains non-exhaustive for a reduction of the number of the variables.

But this proof is easily given. The number of variables can only be reduced by identifying some of the variables of q_1 with some variables occurring in the s_i, or by identifying some of the variables of q_2 with those occurring in the t_k. This must be a tautological transformation; thus the residual of (32) which is true remains true after the transformation. We thus find that for the case $r = 0$ the D-form of p is not exhaustive.

Second, let us assume that the second term of (31) vanishes. Then (31) can be written:

(33) $\qquad ( )...( )[(s_1 \vee ... \vee s_{n-r}).q \vee (s_{n-r+1} \vee ... \vee s_n).(q \vee \bar{q})]$

If q is false, we infer immediately that the first term can be canceled and (33) is not exhaustive. So let us assume that q is true. Before further discussing the form (33) let us consider the possibility that q contains only elementary functions already contained in the s_i; then it might happen that moving the operators of q to the front and reducing the number of variables in q, the resulting elementary terms in the operand q_1 are all identical with those contained in the s_i, so that q_1 would be absorbed in the s_i. In this case, however, there would remain in (33) only terms not containing q, since the tautology $q \lor \bar{q}$ can be canceled, so that q would be shown to be a redundant unit. This case is excluded because it was assumed that p is reduced in the form in which it contains q. Corresponding considerations hold if q includes factors which can be absorbed in the s_i; then these factors would be redundant in p.

So we may assume that the elementary terms contained in q do not vanish even when the operators of q are moved to the front and the number of variables is reduced to a minimum. For this reason, the tautology $q \lor \bar{q}$ in the last term cannot be canceled; the resulting expression would not be a D-form of p, since some of the elementary terms of the first term, namely those contained in q, would not occur in the last term.

Now we can write (33) in the form

$$(34) \qquad (\ )...(\ )[(s_1 \lor ... \lor s_n) . q \lor (s_{n-r+1} \lor ... \lor s_n) . \bar{q}]$$

Using the same methods as described for (32), we can write this

$$(35) \qquad (\ )...(\ )[(s_1 \lor ... \lor s_n) . q_1 \lor (s_{n-r+1} \lor ... \lor s_n) . q_2]$$

and can then conclude that, if q is true, the second term can be canceled, so that the residual

$$(36) \qquad\qquad (\ )...(\ )[(s_1 \lor ... \lor s_n) . q_1]$$

is true.

Reducing the number of variables cannot change this result, except for the possibility of the following manipulation. Instead of going from (33) to (34), we might first replace the tautology $q \lor \bar{q}$ by some other tautology $q \lor q^*$, which possesses the same elementary terms, but where q^* is not the negation of q. (The term q cannot be changed because it is also contained in the first term of (33) and must thus have the same elementary terms and the same operators as q in the latter term; otherwise the number of variables would be increased.) For instance, if q is given as '$(\exists y)h(y)$', the tautology $q \vee \bar{q}$, namely,

$$(37) \qquad (\exists y)h(y) \vee \overline{(\exists y)h(y)}$$

might be replaced by the tautology

$$(38) \qquad (\exists y)h(y) \vee (\exists y)\overline{h(y)}$$

This procedure would in fact reduce the number of variables in (33), when we proceed to the D-form. Instead of (35) we then have the form

$$(39) \qquad (\ )...(\ )[(s_1 \vee ... \vee s_n) \cdot q_1 \vee (s_{n-r+1} \vee ... \vee s_n) \cdot q_2{}^*]$$

where q_2 is the operand contributed by q^* to the D-form. Now we cannot conclude that the second term in (39) is false, because it does not contain the operand q_2, or $\bar{q}$. [1]

This procedure, however, does not make our previous inference invalid, which showed that (36) is true. [2] Now this is a residual of (39), too, and so (39) is not exhaustive. This shows that p is not exhaustive for the case formulated in (33). A similar result is derivable if the first term of (31) vanishes.

Finally, we have to prove that in the general case, when no term of (31) vanishes, p is not exhaustive. This proof is easily given,

---

[1] A D-form of the form (39) may result naturally when p is transformed into D-form directly, without going through the q-expansion. This is always the case when p contains no equivalence operation among its propositional operations. I have constructed a proof for this theorem, but will not give it here, since it is unnecessary for the proof of theorem 5.

[2] This can also be shown as follows. Using the tautology

$$a \cdot q_1 \vee b \cdot q_2{}^* \supset a \vee b$$

we can derive that, if in (39) the factors q_1 and $q_2{}^*$ are canceled, the remaining formula is true. But the content of the brackets then is equivalent to the term in the first parentheses. Therefore, if q is true, (36) is true. The case that q is false was already treated with reference to (33). The transition from (35) to (36) can be proved in the same way.

because either the first or the second term of (31) is false and thus
a residual is true, a result transferred to the D-form. This concludes
the proof of theorem 5.

With the theorems 4–5, the significance of the I-requirements
is made clear. We now turn to the second kind of requirements.

V-Requirements for original nomological statements

1.6. The statement p must be reduced. (Definition 9).

1.7. If p is a disjunction, or if p is a conjunction having a
      major factor p_1 which is a disjunction, then p, or p_1 respec-
      tively, must satisfy the following cancelation condition:
      If one or both of the major terms of p, or of p_1, are trans-
      formed in any way into a conjunction which, taken
      separately, is reduced, then every statement resulting
      from canceling a factor in this conjunction must be reduced.

1.8. If p is an implication, or if p is a conjunction having a
      major factor p_1 which is an implication, then p, or p_1,
      respectively, after being transformed into a disjunction by
      negating the implicans, must satisfy the cancelation con-
      dition of requirement 1.7.

1.9. If p contains an equivalence at any place and this equiv-
      alence is replaced by double implications, the resulting
      statement must satisfy 1.7 and 1.8, with the exception
      that one of the implications may be redundant.

We now introduce the definition:

Definition 27. A statement p is an original nomological
statement if and only if it satisfies the requirements 1.1–1.9.
(V-term).

The significance of requirement 1.6, on the one hand, follows
from the above discussion of reduced statements. This requirement
eliminates unnecessary complications of the form in which the
statement is written. On the other hand, this requirement assumes
an important function through its combination with requirement
1.4: it can be shown that exhaustiveness in major terms, as far as
it is needed, can be derived from this combination. A specific

requirement concerning this kind of exhaustiveness, as was used in ESL, p. 368, is therefore dispensable.

Exhaustiveness in major terms formulates an important requirement for what we call a reasonable use of propositional operations. If a statement is not exhaustive in major terms, its major operation is used inappropriately, because the possibilities opened by it are not exhausted. For instance, consider the two statements:

(40a) $(x)[f(x) \supset g(x)]$

(40b) $(x)(\exists y)[f(x, y) \supset g(x, y)]$

Their expansions in major T-cases have the forms, respectively,

(41a) $(x)[f(x) . g(x) \vee \overline{f(x)} . g(x) \vee \overline{f(x)} . \overline{g(x)}]$

(41b) $(x)(\exists y)[f(x, y) . g(x, y) \vee \overline{f(x, y)} . g(x, y) \vee \overline{f(x, y)} . \overline{g(x, y)}]$

Now assume that the implicans of (40a) is always false, i.e., that the relation holds:

(42a) $(x)\overline{f(x)}$

It was pointed out by Bertrand Russell, as mentioned above, that on this condition the general implication (40a) can lead to unreasonable consequences. For instance, we can thus assert that if x is a centaur x is a banker. When we require that (40a) be exhaustive in major terms, however, the case (42a) is ruled out, because if (42a) were true, we could cancel the first term in the brackets of (41a), while the resulting residual is true.

It is the advantage of the requirement of exhaustiveness that it is applicable to other statement forms where it would not help us to require that the implicans be not always false. For instance, the form (40b) can lead to unreasonable implications of a similar kind as resulting for (40a) even if the implicans of (40b) is not always false. Suppose that '$f(x, y)$' means, 'x is the father of y', and that '$g(x, y)$' means, 'x is taller than y'. In this interpretation, '$f(x, y)$' is not always false. But since here the relation holds

(42b) $(x)(\exists y)\overline{f(x, y)}$

the first term in (41b) can be canceled, and (40b) is therefore not exhaustive in major terms. Thus the form (40b), which in the given interpretation is unreasonable for the very reason that only (42b) makes it true, is ruled out by the requirement of exhaustiveness. This consideration shows that exhaustiveness represents a suitable generalization of Russell's rule according to which an always false implicans should be excluded. Similar considerations apply to the case of an always true implicate. Likewise, the requirement of exhaustiveness can be applied to other propositional operations than implications.

It will now be shown for the individual operations that exhaustiveness in major terms can be derived from requirements 1.4 and 1.6 to a sufficient degree.

Assume, for instance, that in the statement (40a) implicans and implicate are composed of elementary terms, and that the whole statement is exhaustive in elementary terms. Assume further that the implicans is always false, i.e., that (42a) is true. If (42a) is not derivable from (40a), it represents a certain restrictive condition for the elementary terms of (40a) which is added to this statement. But this means that not all elementary T-cases admitted by (40a) are satisfiable, and thus (40a) is not exhaustive in elementary terms. Therefore, (42a) must be derivable from (40a). Since, vice versa, (40a) is derivable from (42a), both statements are tautologically equivalent. Consequently, (40a) is not reduced; namely, we can cancel the implicate when we add a negation line on the implicans. (Definition 7 for synthetic, definition 8 for analytic statements.)

In a similar way we can prove that (40a) is not reduced if the implicate is always true. Canceling the implicans in (40a), we then arrive at a tautologically equivalent form.

With respect to exhaustiveness in major terms, these two cases are classified as follows, when we refer to the expansion in major T-cases given by (41a). If (40a) has an always false implicans, the first term in the brackets of (41a) can be canceled. If (40a) has an always true implicate, the last term in the brackets of (41a) can be canceled. These are the two cases already discussed. It remains to discuss the case that the middle term in (41a) can be canceled. However, it is unnecessary to discuss the possibility that two terms in (41a) can be canceled, because this leads back to the first two cases. For instance, if the last two terms in (41a) can be canceled, we can reduce (40a) by canceling the implicans. Since we can go from '$g(x)$' to '$f(x) \supset g(x)$', we can rederive (40a), and since this statement was assumed to imply the considered residual of (41a), we thus derive '$(x)f(x).g(x)$'. This shows that here the latter statement is replaceable by the reduced form of (40a).

Now if the middle term in (41a) is dispensable, the implication can be replaced by an equivalence. Here the implication (40a) is reduced, because it cannot be transformed into an equivalence by canceling terms. It cannot even be written as double implication, because the converse implication is then redundant, being derivable from the first implication; this derivability follows similarly as was explained for (42a).

With respect to this converse implication we have to distinguish two cases, according as this implication is synthetic or tautological. An example of the first kind is given by the statement

$$(43) \qquad (x)(y)[f(x, y) \supset f(y, x)]$$

from which we can operator-derive the converse implication by interchanging 'x' and 'y'. If we add this implication, and write

$$(43a) \qquad (x)(y)\{[f(x, y) \supset f(y, x)].[f(y, x) \supset f(x, y)]\}$$

this statement is not reduced, because the second brackets can be canceled. So it appears reasonable to accept (43), which is reduced. This statement is exhaustive in major terms *except for itself*, because the statements p_1 and p of definition 19 here coincide. The exclusion of a major T-case is here acceptable because it is said by the statement itself. An illustration of (43) is given by the statement: 'if x is a sibling of y, then y is a sibling of x'. We do not hesitate to accept this implication as reasonable although it can be replaced by an 'if and only if', i.e., by a double implication or an equivalence. Note that (43), if the terms '$f(x, y)$' and '$f(y, x)$' are elementary terms, is exhaustive in elementary terms, because definition 16 refers to the complete matrix of the statement, given here by (43a). In contrast, exhaustiveness in major terms refers to the form (43), in which the statement is given.

An example where the converse implication is tautological is given by the statement

(44) $(x)[f(x) \vee g(x) \supset f(x) . g(x)]$

Here, too, we cannot add the converse implication because the statement then would not be reduced. But since this converse implication is tautological, it can be said to be derivable from the statement itself; thus (44) is exhaustive in major terms except for itself. An example is given by the statement: 'if one of two condenser plates is electrically charged, then both are electrically charged'.

There is an essential difference between these forms and the forms discussed previously, in which the falsehood of the implicans, or the truth of the implicate, can be derived from the statement itself. The implication which is replaceable by an equivalence, exemplified by (43) and (44), is both reduced and exhaustive in major terms except for itself. However, the implication with an always false implicans, or an always true implicate, though exhaustive in major terms except for itself, is not reduced. We see that the combination of the two conditions, being reduced and being exhaustive in major terms, except for itself, guarantees a form of implication which we are willing to accept as reasonable. But the latter condition is derivable from exhaustiveness in elementary terms; therefore, the combination of requirements 1.4 and 1.6 furnishes precisely the kind of implication which we are willing to accept.

For these reasons, the requirement of exhaustiveness in major terms, used in ESL, p. 369, can be dropped. Its function is taken over by the requirement that the statement must be reduced, though in a more tolerant way. For implications — and the other operations will be discussed presently — this means: when 'if and only if' is the grammatical conjunction that makes the statement exhaustive in major terms, the form 'if' is still admitted. This is one of the changes of the present theory as compared with that of ESL. Only the cases of an always false implicans and an always true implicate are still excluded, both for synthetic and analytic statements. We may add that, when '$f(x)$' and '$g(x)$' are elementary terms in (40a), (this can only occur in synthetic statements), the requirement 1.4 of exhaustiveness in elementary terms directly rules out forms in which the implicans is always false or the implicate is always true; here the requirement of being reduced is not applicable and not necessary. And it then cannot happen that the converse implication of (40a) is derivable from (40a) or is tautological, because this would require a substructure of the terms. For this reason, a synthetic implication like (40a) which could be replaced by an equivalence is not accepted as an original nomological statement if the terms '$f(x)$' and '$g(x)$' are elementary terms. Such implications, however, will be admitted later into a somewhat wider category (see the discussion following theorem 13).

It is different when the implication is analytic. The implication

$$(45) \qquad\qquad (x)[f(x) \supset f(x)]$$

satisfies all requirements 1.1–1.9, even if '$f(x)$' is an elementary term. In particular, it is exhaustive in elementary terms, since it has only one elementary term; and it is reduced. Its dispensable major T-case (which is not an elementary T-case) '$\overline{f(x)}.f(x)$' is contradictory; thus the corresponding residual is tautological and can be regarded as derivable from the statement itself. Statement (45) is therefore exhaustive in major terms except for itself. Because of the satisfaction of the requirements 1.1–1.9, statement (45) is an original nomological statement.

It will now be shown that similar considerations can be carried through for the other operations, if they stand in the major place. We begin with the inclusive 'or'. Assume that in the statement

$$(46) \qquad\qquad (x)[f(x) \vee g(x)]$$

the major terms stand for combinations of elementary terms, and assume further that the statement is exhaustive in these elementary terms. If the statement remains true when one of the terms is canceled, the resulting statement must be derivable from (46), because otherwise it would represent an additional condition for the elementary terms and make (46) nonexhaustive in elementary terms. But if one term can be canceled, (46) is not reduced, whether it is synthetic or analytic. There remains the possibility that the 'or' in

(46) can be replaced by the exclusive 'or', i.e. ,that we can add to the operand of (46) the relation $'\overline{f(x)} \vee \overline{g(x)}'$. If (46) is exhaustive in elementary terms, this relation must be derivable from (46); so if we add it, the resulting statement would not be reduced. But in this case, at least, (46) is reduced. Although it might then appear preferable to write (46) with the sign of the exclusive 'or', we would not object to using an inclusive 'or' when we know from the statement itself that it can be replaced by an exclusive 'or'. For instance, we are willing to accept such statements as 'a comet moves on an open or a closed conic section', even when the 'or' is not expressly marked to be exclusive. In this example, the relation that can be added, namely, $'\overline{f(x)} \vee \overline{g(x)}'$, would be tautological; in other examples it will be synthetic, though derivable from (46).

For the equivalence as major operation, the situation is slightly different. In order to exclude unreasonable forms, requirement 1.8 has been added. Consider the statement

(47) $$(x)[f(x) \equiv g(x)]$$

and assume that the two terms stand for certain combinations of elementary terms. If (47) is not exhaustive in major terms, but is exhaustive in elementary terms, then either $'f(x).g(x)'$ or $'\overline{f(x)}.\overline{g(x)}'$ is dispensable. Assume the latter is the case; then we can replace the brackets in (47) by the combination $'f(x).g(x)'$. When we now write (47) in the form

(48) $$(x)\{[f(x) \supset g(x)].[g(x) \supset f(x)]\}$$

we see that neither of these implications is reduced, because their implicans can be canceled. For the other case an analogous result can be proved. Thus requirement 1.8 makes it impossible to use an equivalence as major operation if it is not exhaustive in major terms.

If one of the implications in (48) is tautological, or derivable from the other, while this other one is synthetic, (48) is not reduced. For this case, requirement 1.8 admits the form (47), which is reduced and exhaustive except for itself. If the implicational form is used, the redundant implication in (48) is to be canceled. Examples are given by (43) and (45). In both these instances it would be permissible to replace the implication by an equivalence.

Finally, if the 'and' is the major operation, it is always exhaustive in major terms, because it has only one T-case. We do not consider here the exclusive 'or', because a special sign for this operation is seldom used. If it were to be used, a special requirement by analogy with 1.8 would have to be introduced, demanding that the statement be reduced if the exclusive 'or' is replaced by a conjunction of two inclusive disjunctions, in the form '$(a \vee b).(\bar{a} \vee \bar{b})$'.

These results may be summarized in the following theorem, which holds both for synthetic and for analytic statements:

Theorem 6. If a statement is original-nomological, it is exhaustive in major terms except for itself. Thus the only cases where the statement can be non-exhaustive in major terms are the following ones: the statement may be an implication which can be replaced by an equivalence; or it may be an inclusive disjunction which can be replaced by an exclusive one.

These considerations show that the major operations of original nomological statements are used in a way we regard as reasonable. They apply likewise when the operation occurs as the major operation of a major factor of a conjunction which is original-nomological, because the given proofs can be constructed for each such factor separately. However, an important distinction is to be made. If the conjunction is exhaustive in elementary terms, we cannot infer that each factor is so, although each factor is asserted as true and the concept of exhaustiveness is at least applicable. But we can conclude that each factor is exhaustive in elementary terms except for the total statement (definition 19). Going through the previous proofs with this qualification, we find that the cases where the statement is not reduced are the same as before; but for the two cases where the converse implication, or the exclusiveness of the disjunction, is derivable, we find that these relations are derivable, not from the factor alone, but only from the total statement. This result is transferred to major terms. Consider, for instance, the statement

(49) $$(x)\{[f(x) \supset g(x)].[g(x) \supset f(x)]\}$$

in which the given terms may be elementary or stand for combinations of elementary terms. When we take the first implication alone, it is not exhaustive in major terms except for itself, but only except for the total statement. We can still accept such implications as reasonable if they are used in the context of the total statement. We shall later study this kind of statement in more detail (see definition 34).

An illustration where the equivalence operation occurs in major factors is given by the formulation of an exclusive disjunction of three terms (see ESL, p. 45):

$$(50) \qquad (x)\{[f_1(x) \equiv \overline{f_2(x)} \cdot \overline{f_3(x)}] \cdot [f_2(x) \equiv \overline{f_1(x)} \cdot \overline{f_3(x)}]\}$$

In contrast to (49), this statement cannot be replaced by a single equivalence. Neither factor of (50) is exhaustive in the given terms, but either one is exhaustive except for the total statement. The statement (50) is original-nomological; and it remains so if the equivalences are replaced by double implications. We arrive at the following theorem:

Theorem 7. If a conjunction is original-nomological, each factor is exhaustive in major and elementary terms except for the total statement. Thus the only cases where a factor can be non-exhaustive in major terms are the following ones: the factor may be an implication which can be replaced by an equivalence; or it may be an inclusive disjunction which can be replaced by an exclusive one.

Summarizing, we may say that propositional operations can be called reasonable when they stand as major operations of original nomological statements, or as major operations of major factors of such statements. To go beyond this result and define reasonable operations for secondary places of a statement, appears extremely difficult. Though the requirement of being reduced controls every unit within the statement (theorem 1), it is not sufficient if it is not combined with the requirement of exhaustiveness. But the units in which secondary operations occur are not asserted as true; therefore the criterion of exhaustiveness is not applicable, being defined for true statements only (definitions 16 and 18).

I have made many attempts to generalize this requirement in

such a way that every operation within a statement is made reasonable; but this aim seems unattainable. Consider, for instance, an implication in a secondary place, i.e., standing as the implicate of a major implication. It is not asserted to be true, since its truth depends on the major implicans. But how could we characterize an implication as reasonable without assuming that it is true? The methods used for the definition of nomological statements certainly could not be used, because they presuppose truth of the statement in an essential manner. A false implication cannot be reasonable. Or assume that the statement consists in a negated implication. Then the negation is the major operation and thus is a connective operation; but the implication is not. It is merely a negated adjunctive implication. The negation of a connective implication would be something very different (see ESL, p. 380).

It will be shown in chapter 8 that for certain special cases, at least, secondary operations can be made reasonable in a somewhat wider sense; they are then called relative nomological operations. For instance, a secondary implication can be made reasonable for the case that it is true, and thus for the case that the major implicans is true. However, within the theory of absolute, or unconditional, nomological statements, with which we are concerned in the present and the following two chapters, the only way to improve the status of secondary operations is to strengthen the methods of reducing. Whether a unit is reduced depends often on the statement in which it is imbedded. Therefore, rules for stronger methods of reducing have been formulated in requirements 1.7–1.9, which must now be studied. Let us use an implication for an illustration:

(51) $$(x)[f_1(x) \lor f_2(x) \supset g_1(x) . g_2(x)]$$

Here the four terms written down may be elementary or stand for combinations of elementary terms. Negating the implicans we have

(51a) $$(x)[\overline{f_1(x)} . \overline{f_2(x)} \lor g_1(x) . g_2(x)]$$

When we now cancel factors according to requirement 1.7 and transform the resulting disjunction into implications we obtain four implications of the form

(51b) $$(x)[f_i(x) \supset g_k(x)] \qquad i, k = 1, 2$$

Requirements 1.7–1.8 guarantee that these four implications, whose conjunction is equivalent to (51), are reduced; they thus satisfy theorem 7, and can be accepted as reasonable. This result, conversely, makes the 'or' in the implicans of (51) reasonable. And if this implicans is written in the form '$\overline{f_1(x)} \supset f_2(x)$', this secondary implication appears thus reasonable to a certain degree.

Another illustration is given by the statement of an implied equivalence, or double implication:

$$(52) \qquad (x)\{f(x) \supset [g(x) \supset h(x)] . [h(x) \supset g(x)]\}$$

If this implication satisfies requirement 1.8, each implication resulting from canceling one of the brackets is reasonable in the sense explained previously.

An example which violates 1.8 is given by the statement

$$(53) \qquad (x)[\overline{f(x)} \lor g(x) \supset f(x) . h(x)]$$

This statement is exhaustive in major and elementary terms, and it is reduced. But if we cancel the term '$h(x)$', the resulting statement is not reduced, because it is equivalent to the statement '$(x)f(x)$'. Thus requirement 1.8 rules out unreasonable forms like (53), which the other requirements do not eliminate. Note that (53) is also ruled out if the implicans is written in the form '$f(x) \supset g(x)$', because requirements 1.7–1.8 refer to possible transformations of the major terms; thus this secondary implication is regarded as unreasonable. In this manner, requirements 1.7–1.8, in achieving a certain mutual reducing of implicans and implicate, contribute to the reasonableness of secondary operations.

An illustration of (53) is given, when we use for '$g(x)$' a negative form, by the statement 'if masses do not have attractive forces or galaxies do not recede, then masses have attractive forces and galaxies have an enormous gravitational potential'. This statement satisfies all the requirements 1.1–1.6, but violates 1.8. Note that the statement is ruled out by 1.7 if the implication is converted into a disjunction: 'masses have attractive forces and galaxies recede, or masses have attractive forces and galaxies have an enormous gravitational potential'. The duplication of the first part is here regarded as an unnecessary complication.

The reducing process required by 1.7–1.9 can of course always be carried out. The terms violating these requirements are not redundant; but they can be canceled if they are added, in suitable form, outside the implication. For instance, (53) then assumes the form

(53a) $$(x)\{[g(x) \supset h(x)] . f(x)\}$$

This form is equivalent to (53) and satisfies requirements 1.6–1.8. The sentence used for the illustration would thus read: 'masses have attractive forces, and galaxies recede or have an enormous gravitational potential'.

IV

DERIVATIVE NOMOLOGICAL STATEMENTS

We now turn to derivative nomological statements, beginning with the definition:

Definition 28. A statement is *nomological*, also called *nomological in the wider sense*, if it is deductively derivable from a set of original nomological statements. The major operation of a nomological statement is called a *connective operation*. (*I*-terms).

Definition 28 is the same as given in ESL, p. 371. But since definition 27 lays down narrower rules for original nomological statements than does the corresponding definition given in ESL, p. 371, requirements 1.5–1.9 being added, both the classes of original nomological statements and of nomological statements are narrowed down. However, as in the previous presentation, the class of nomological statements includes all tautologies. In particular, tautologies written in the calculus of propositions are introduced with definition 28 into the class of derivative nomological statements. They are not original nomological statements because they possess no all-operators; but they result from tautologies containing all-operators and satisfying the requirements for original nomological statements by a derivation process in which functionals are replaced by constants. [1]

A nomological statement may violate the requirements 1.2–1.9, but it cannot violate requirement 1.1, since it is verifiably true. Dropping of major all-operators and transition to free variables is regarded as abandoning requirement 1.3; statements thus resulting are nomological, but not original-nomological.

Some remarks about conjunctions must now be added. If two original nomological statements p and q, which are synthetic, are combined into the conjunction $p.q$, this conjunction, though nomological, need not be original-nomological. A set of original

---

[1] See ESL, p. 139, rule (a).

nomological statements is not always equivalent to one original
nomological statement, though it is equivalent to a nomological
statement, namely, to the conjunction of the statements of the set.
However, it will now be shown that this conjunction deviates from
an original nomological statement only in minor points, and that it
can be replaced by an original nomological statement (theorem 9).

It is easily seen that requirements 1.1–1.3 and 1.7–1.9 are
satisfied by the conjunction. We shall now show that requirement
1.5 is satisfied by the conjunction.

Let two original nomological statements be given; we write them
in C-form (definition 10):

$$(54) \qquad (\ )...(\ )[(e_1 \vee ... \vee e_m)_1 ..... (e_1 \vee ... \vee e_m)_\mu]$$

$$(55) \qquad (\ )...(\ )[(e_1' \vee ... \vee e_k')_1 ..... (e_1' \vee ... \vee e_k')_\nu]$$

In the parentheses, some of the elementary terms occur in negated
form; instead of writing corresponding negation lines, we have
added subscripts to the parentheses, so that each subscript indicates
a particular combination of positive and negative elementary terms.
Some of the elementary terms of (55) may be identical with elementary terms of (54). We now write the conjunction of the two
statements in one-scope form, as follows. Argument variables
governed by all-operators are given the same names in both statements, as far as this is possible; however, variables governed by
existential operators in (55) are given names different from those
of the existential variables in (54). We thus arrive at the form:

$$(56) (\ )...(\ )[(e_1 \vee ... \vee e_m)_1 ..... (e_1 \vee ... \vee e_m)_\mu . (e_1' \vee ... \vee e_k')_1 ..... (e_1' \vee ... \vee e_k')_\nu]$$

This is not a C-form, but a shorter conjunctive normal form. Yet
if (54) and (55) satisfy requirement 1.5, (56) cannot possess a self-
contained conjunctive residual which is purely existential. Such
a residual can only result when, by the use of relations (19), certain
factors merge in such a way that terms containing variables
governed by all-operators drop out. But since either (54) or (55)
contains at least one existential operator — otherwise (56) could
not have an existential residual — the elementary terms stemming
from one formula cannot be throughout the same as those stemming

from the other formula, because existential variables in the two formulae have different names.

However, it may be possible to overcome this difference by merging of variables, using such tautologies as

(57) $\qquad (\exists y)(x)f(x, y) \equiv (\exists y)(x)f(x, x) . f(y, y)$

(58) $\qquad (\exists x)(Ey)f(x) . f(y) . p \equiv (\exists x)f(x) . p$

(59) $\qquad (\exists x)(\exists y)[a \vee g(x) . p] . [\bar{a} \vee g(y) . p] \equiv (\exists x)g(x) . p$

By the use of such formulae, it may be possible to transform (56) equivalently into a form in which at least one statement contains a smaller number of elementary terms, so that we arrive at the form

(60) $\qquad \begin{array}{l} \big\langle \ (\ )\ldots(\ )[(e_1 \vee \ldots \vee e_{m-s})_1 . \ldots . (e_1 \vee \ldots \vee e_{m-s})_{\mu-\varrho} \\ \big\langle \ . (e_1' \vee \ldots \vee e_{k-t}')_1 . \ldots . (e_1' \vee \ldots \vee e_{k-t}')]_{\nu-\sigma} \end{array}$

This statement, in which $s > 0$ or $t > 0$ or both, may possess a self-contained conjunctive residual which is purely existential.

To have an illustration for elimination of elementary terms, consider the two statements

(61) $\qquad (x)(\exists y)[f(x, y) \vee g(y)]$

(62) $\qquad (x) \ (y) \ [\overline{f(x, y)} \vee g(y)]$

Their conjunction is in one-scope form

(63) $\qquad (x)(\exists y)(z)[f(x, y) \vee g(y)] . [\overline{f(x, z)} \vee g(z)]$

Using the tautology (57) and putting there 'z' for 'x', we see that (63) is equivalent to

(64) $\qquad (x)(\exists y)(z)[\overline{f(x, y)} \vee g(y)] . [f(x, y) \vee g(y)] . [\overline{f(x, z)} \vee g(z)]$

Here the first brackets represent a factor not contained in (63), and this factor merges with the second factor in such a way that we arrive at the following statement, which is equivalent to (63)

(65) $\qquad (x)(\exists y)(z)\{g(y) . [\overline{f(x, z)} \vee g(z)]\}$

Whereas (63), in the form written, does not possess any self-contained conjunctive residual which is purely existential, the equivalent form (65) does possess such a residual, namely, the part

'$(\exists y)g(y)$'. Therefore, (63) is not general in self-contained factors. The latter term was defined in definition 23 in such a way that it refers to the complete matrix of a statement; this follows because the term 'conjunctive residual' used in definition 23 refers to the C-form of a statement. Since (65) is not propositionally derivable from (63), but merely operator-derivable (see the discussion of (12) and (14)), (63) does not contain the complete matrix of the statement. Although even (65) does not represent the complete matrix of (63), it shows already the existence of a conjunctive residual contrary to definition 23.

Now it is easily seen that (61) is not exhaustive, because its disjunctive residual '$(\exists y)g(y)$' is true. Therefore, (65) does not represent a conjunction of two original nomological statements. We shall now show that whenever, the conjunction can be given a form like (65), at least one of the individual statements is not exhaustive.

This is shown as follows. In the transformation leading from (56) to (60) we follow the rule always to keep the statement in one scope form; furthermore, if operators become redundant, we do not cancel them. Then the operator set remains the same on each step; and since we use only equivalent transformations, each step represents an equivalent version of the original conjunction. Now there must be one step (or several) on which through merging of variables a factor is produced which contains only such elementary terms as occur in the first (or second) formula, as for instance on the step (64), where the first brackets represent such an emergent term. The statement (56) thus is equivalently transformed into

$$(66) \quad ( )...( )[(e_1 \vee ... \vee e_m)_1 \cdot ..... (e_1 \vee ... \vee e_m)_\mu \cdot (e_1 \vee ... \vee e_m)_{\mu+1} \\ \cdot (e_1' \vee ... \vee e_k')_1 \cdot ..... (e_1' \vee ... \vee e_k')']$$

When we cancel here the factors containing terms with prime marks, we derive a statement which after canceling redundant operators has the operator set of (54). But this statement is a conjunctive extension of (54), and according to the remarks following definition 21, is thus equivalent to a disjunctive residual of (54). We thus have shown that a disjunctive residual of (54) is true, or in other words, that (54) is not exhaustive in elementary terms.

The proof is easily extended to a conjunction of three or more statements, because there must always be a step on which a certain factor is added to one of the statements in such a way that a certain elementary term drops out; through this addition, a conjunctive extension of that statement is derived. Therefore, we have the following theorem:

Theorem 8. If a conjunction of two or more synthetic statements is not general in self-contained factors, whereas each statement is so, then at least one of the statements is not exhaustive in elementary terms.

This theorem is of great importance within the theory of synthetic nomological statements. It shows that a conjunction of original nomological statements cannot violate requirement 1.5. If the theorem were not true, we could transcribe any purely existential statement into a conjunction of original nomological statements, and thus make the existential statement nomological. For instance, in (65) the part '$(\exists y)g(y)$' might mean 'there exists copper', whereas the other part may be given any suitable interpretation by a true statement. Then the statements (61) and (62) would be true, being derivable form (65), and they would thus be original nomological statements. In this way, the statement 'there exists copper' would be made a law of nature. Such a procedure is excluded by theorem 6. In our example, the procedure breaks down because (61) is not exhaustive and thus not original-nomological.

The only requirements which a conjunction of original nomological statements can violate are requirements 1.4 and 1.6. The latter possibility is obvious; for instance, the two statements may have a common factor, which would be redundant in their conjunction. But it is of course always possible to reduce the conjunction, for instance, by canceling the common factor once.

That a conjunction of two original nomological statements, though exhaustive in major terms, need not be exhaustive in elementary terms, is shown by the following example. Consider the two statements

(67a) $\qquad\qquad (x)[f(x) \supset g(x)]$

(67b) $\qquad\qquad (x)[h(x) \supset k(x)]$

They may be original-nomological. Assume that furthermore the relation holds

(67c) $$(x)[f(x) \supset \overline{h(x)}]$$

Then the conjunction of the statements (67a–b) is not exhaustive in elementary terms.

However, this deficiency can be remedied. We have merely to add, to the conjunction of the statements, the condition which establishes a relation between the elementary terms; then the resulting statement is exhaustive in elementary terms. In the example given we thus construct the conjunction of the three statements (67a–c), which is original-nomological. It is not always possible to make the addition in the form of a separate statement; if the two original nomological statements possess existential operators, it may be necessary to make the addition directly to the operand of the one-scope form of their conjunction. We thus arrive at the theorem:

Theorem 9. A conjunction of two synthetic original nomological statements either is original-nomological, or can be made so by adding some part and reducing.

Thus far we have studied the transition from two original nomological statements to their conjunction. Considering the converse transition, we see easily that if a synthetic conjunction is original-nomological, its factors need not be so. But from theorem 7 we know that its factors are, at least, reasonable to some degree, being exhaustive except for the total conjunction. A study of this property may be postponed to the discussion of definition 35.

V

ADMISSIBLE STATEMENTS

We now introduce a new notation, in which an order of truth is defined, and which will be useful for our further investigations.

Definition 29. A tautology is *true of third order*; a synthetic nomological statement is *true of second order*; a statement which is verifiably true but not nomological, is *true of first order*. If p is true of k-th order, $\bar{p}$ is false of k-th order. (I-terms).

Note that the second-order character is not restricted to original nomological statements, but also applies to all derivative nomological statements. Likewise, the class of third-order statements includes both those tautologies which are original-nomological and those which are not.

Definition 30. A *set of statements* has the order of the lowest-order statements contained in it. (I-term).

Theorem 10. A true statement has the order of the highest-order sets from which it is derivable.

This theorem follows immediately from the nature of analytic and synthetic statements, and from definitions 29–30.

It was shown in ESL, § 65, that nomological statements can be used to define modalities. This chapter of my previous theory remains unchanged, when the new definition of original nomological statements is assumed for it and it is thus referred to the new class of nomological statements. However, it was also pointed out that for the definition of reasonable operations, the class of nomological statements is too wide, while the class of original nomological statements is too narrow. For this reason, an intermediate class of nomological statements in the narrower sense was defined in ESL, p. 371. This definition will now be changed, for the reasons explained above. The new intermediate class, which is less comprehensive than the older one, will likewise be called *nomological in the narrower sense*; in order to have a brief name, we shall speak of *admissible statements.* This class is subdivided into the two classes of *fully admissible* and *semi-admissible* statements, which will be defined in order. The term 'admissible operation', which refers to the major operations of both subclasses, is proposed as the explicans of the vague term 'reasonable operation'.

The definition will again be given by means of I-requirements and V-requirements. First, some new terms must be defined.

Definition 31. A statement p which is true of the order k is *quasi-exhaustive* (in major or in elementary terms) if none of its disjunctive residuals (in major or in elementary terms) is true of an order $\geq k$. (I-term for elementary terms, V-term for major terms.)

It is not necessary here to write 'verifiably true', because the qualifier 'verifiably' is already included in the definition of 'true of the order k'. Note that a statement which is exhaustive is also quasi-exhaustive.

Definition 32. A statement p, which is true of the order k is *quasi-exhaustive except for p* (in major or elementary terms) if none of its disjunctive residuals is derivable from p, but all those of its disjunctive residuals which are true of an order $\geq k$ are derivable from p. (I-term for elementary terms, V-term for major terms.)

Note that a statement which is quasi-exhaustive is also quasi-exhaustive except for p, for any p.

We now proceed to the definition of fully admissible statements, introducing the following I-requirements.

I-REQUIREMENTS FOR FULLY ADMISSIBLE STATEMENTS

2.1. The statement p must be deductively derivable from a set of original nomological statements.

2.2. The statement p must be quasi-exhaustive in elementary terms. (Definition 31).

It is not necessary to introduce specific V-requirements; we simply take over the V-requirements of original nomological statements, i.e., requirements 1.6–1.9. We thus define:

Definition 33. A statement p is *fully admissible* if it satisfies requirements 2.1–2.2 and 1.6–1.9. The major operation of a fully admissible statement is called a *fully admissible* operation. (V-terms).

It is easily seen from the remarks added to definition 31 that every original nomological statement is fully admissible. The subclass of fully admissible statements which are not original-nomological will be called *fully admissible by derivation*.

The use of the concept 'quasi-exhaustive' is seen in its application to implications. If '$a \supset b$' is true of second order, while 'a' is false of first order, the implication, though not exhaustive, is reasonable, being quasi-exhaustive. Of this kind are the usual conditionals contrary to fact. 'If there had been a current in the high voltage wire, the man who touched the wire would have been killed.' The implicans refers here merely to a matter of fact which did not occur, whereas the implication expresses a physical law.

In contrast, an unreasonable implication can be constructed as follows. If 'a' and 'b' are true of the 2nd order, '$a \supset b$' is also of 2nd order, being derivable from 'a' and 'b'. But '$a \supset b$' is not quasi-exhaustive, because its residual 'b', which is the same as '$a.b \lor \bar{a}.b$', is true of the same order as '$a \supset b$'. It is different when '$a \supset b$' is true of 3rd order, while 'a' and 'b' are of 2nd order; then '$a \supset b$' is quasi-exhaustive and, if also the further requirements are satisfied, nomological in the restricted sense. A tautological implication between synthetic nomological statements is thus considered as reasonable. For instance, the implication, 'if Newton's law of gravitation holds, Kepler's laws of planetary motion are true', appears reasonable. An unreasonable implication is given by the statement, 'if Newton's law of gravitation holds, Ohm's law of electric circuits is true'. This implication, though nomological because derivable from the truth of these laws taken separately, is not quasi-exhaustive, since it is of the same order as its implicate, and thus is not admitted as reasonable.

It will be shown presently that for tautologies the class of semi-admissible statements is empty; therefore, the terms *admissible* and *fully admissible* coincide for tautologies. However, not all tautologies are admissible. Now requirements 2.1 and 2.2 are always satisfied for tautologies, the latter requirement because canceling a term in the D-form leads to a synthetic and thus to a lower-order statement. This holds, too, when the tautology is specialized. Therefore, only the V-requirements 1.6–1.9 select, among the tautologies, the admissible ones. Note that conjunctions of tautologies are never admissible, because they are not reduced (definition 8); the same holds for a conjunction of a synthetic statement with a tautology (definition 7). Examples of inadmissible and admissible tautologies are given on the left-hand sides and right-hand sides of (8)–(10), respectively.

In the discussion of the forms (50)–(60) it was shown that for reduced statements the requirement of exhaustiveness in elementary terms leads to the consequence that these statements are exhaustive in major terms to a sufficient extent. It is easily seen that similar conclusions can be drawn with respect to quasi-exhaustiveness. If there exists a relation of the same order as, or of a higher order than, the statement, and if this relation restricts the major terms, it must be derivable from the statement, because otherwise it would also restrict the elementary terms, and thus the statement would not be quasi-exhaustive in elementary terms. For these reasons, we can derive the following analogues of the theorems 6–7, which again hold both for synthetic and for analytic statements:

Theorem 11. If a statement is fully admissible, it is quasi-exhaustive in major terms except for itself. Thus the only cases where the statement can be non-quasi-exhaustive in major terms are the following ones: the statement may be an implication which can be replaced by an equivalence; or it may be an inclusive disjunction which can be replaced by an exclusive one.

Theorem 12. If a conjunction is fully admissible, each factor is quasi-exhaustive in major and elementary terms except for the total statement. Thus the only cases where a factor can be non-quasi-exhaustive in major terms are the following ones: the factor may be an implication which can be replaced by an equivalence; or it may be an inclusive disjunction which can be replaced by an exclusive one.

The synthetic implications accepted by theorem 11 as fully admissible resemble as to their structure those admitted by theorem 6 into original nomological statements. In particular, a synthetic implication which can be replaced by an equivalence can be fully admissible only if its major terms are compound; if they are elementary terms, such an implication is still ruled out. These implications will be admitted later (see the discussion following theorem 13). In contrast, it was explained for formula (45) that analytic implications of this kind are accepted. In addition to statement (45), which is original-nomological, we accept as fully admissible the form '$a \supset a$', which because of its missing all-operator is not original-nomological.

We now turn to the definition of semi-admissible statements, for which purpose we introduce the following definitions and requirements. These statements are distinguished from fully admissible ones in that they are not quasi-exhaustive in elementary terms; i.e., requirement 2.2 is abandoned. Of this kind are certain statements referred to in the last theorem. In contrast to original nomological statements, the V-requirements 1.6–1.9 are not sufficient for semi-admissible statements. We need certain requirements concerning quasi-exhaustiveness in major terms, which is no longer derivable when 2.2 is given up.

Definition 34. If a nomological statement p is not quasi-exhaustive in major terms except for itself, it is called *supplementable* if it can be made, without any change, a factor in a reduced conjunction such that p is quasi-exhaustive in major terms except for the conjunction. (V-term).

Of the following requirements, 1.10* has no analogue among previous requirements. In contrast, 1.7*–1.9* are merely stronger forms of the corresponding requirements 1.7–1.9.

V-REQUIREMENTS FOR SEMI-ADMISSIBLE STATEMENTS

1.7*.   The statements described in the cancellation condition of requirement 1.7 must not only be reduced, but must also be quasi-exhaustive in major terms, or be so except for themselves, or be supplementable.

1.8*.   The statements described in requirement 1.8 must not only satisfy requirements 1.6–1.7, but also 1.7*.

1.9*.   The statements described in requirement 1.9 must not only satisfy requirements 1.6–1.8, but also 1.7*–1.8*.

1.10*. The statement p must either be quasi-exhaustive in major terms, or be so except for itself, or be supplementable into a conjunction which satisfies 1.6, 1.7*–1.10*, 2.1.

In the following definition, the term *non-conjunctive* refers to statements, or to factors in a conjunction, which do not have a conjunction as their major operation.

Definition 35. A non-conjunctive statement p is *semi-admissible* if it satisfies requirements 1.6, 1.7*–1.10*, 2.1 but is not fully admissible. A conjunction p is *semi-admissible* if it satisfies requirement 1.6 and each of its non-conjunctive factors is semi-admissible but not fully admissible. The major operation of a semi-admissible statement is called a *semi-admissible operation*. (V-term).

It is easily seen that requirements 1.7*–1.10* are always satisfied by fully admissible statements; this follows from theorems 11–12. However, according to definition 35, fully admissible statements are not semi-admissible, the latter class being defined so as to exclude the former. The use of the new requirements for semi-admissible statements will be illustrated presently.

The concept of semi-admissibility applies only to synthetic statements, because tautologies always satisfy requirement 2.2. For synthetic statements, the introduction of the wider category of semi-admissible statements appears advisable for the following reasons. Exhaustiveness in elementary terms is used for original nomological statements essentially to eliminate forms containing closed existential units (theorem 5). Once the class of original nomological statements has been defined, the class of nomological statements does not need such a protection, because these statements are sufficiently protected by the requirement of being derivable from original nomological ones. For admissible statements, quasi-exhaustiveness in elementary terms serves mainly to ensure the corresponding property for major terms to a sufficient extent. If, however, the latter property is guaranteed by other means, the possibility arises to renounce quasi-exhaustiveness in elementary terms completely.

Consider, for instance, the statement, 'if a metal is heated, it expands'. We symbolized it in propositional variables, because operators are not required for derivative nomological statements,

and can be dispensed with for the following considerations. It then
has the form

(68) $a \supset b$

From it we can derive the statement, 'if a metal is heated and is
red, it expands', to be symbolized

(69) $a.c \supset b$

This implication, which like (68) is true of second order, is not
quasi-exhaustive in elementary terms, because relation (68) excludes
the T-case '$a.\bar{c}.\bar{b}$' as being false of second order. When we are still
willing to accept (69) as reasonable, this may be accounted for by
the fact that (69) is quasi-exhaustive in major terms, because the
major T-case '$\overline{a.c}.\bar{b}$' is not false of second order; the implicans
can be made false by making 'a' false. For this reason, (69) satisfies
requirement 1.10* and is semi-admissible. The slightly disparaging
connotation of the latter term may reflect the feeling of uneasiness
we have about this implication, which contains the unnecessary
reference to the color of the metal. A technical reason for setting
off this category from that of fully admissible statements will turn
up presently.

A somewhat more general case than (69) is given when the
statement is merely quasi-exhaustive in major terms except for
itself. An illustration may be constructed from (43) by assuming
that the interpretations of the terms '$f(x, y)$' and '$f(y, x)$' of this
statement are composed of elementary terms in such a way that
the statement is not exhaustive in them.

In order to construct an example for the most general case,
consider the statement: 'a living organism receives energy from
digesting remnants of other organisms, or it is a plant and receives
energy from direct assimilation of light'. The 'or' is here inclusive,
because there are insect catching plants which do both. The statement is symbolized in propositional variables

(70) $a \supset b \vee c.d$

Each propositional variable stands here for a certain compound
structure of elementary terms. But we need not introduce these

elementary terms in order to see that (70) is not quasi-exhaustive in elementary terms, because the relation holds

(70a) $$c \equiv d$$

which restricts the elementary terms, but is not derivable from (70). Furthermore, in the given interpretation, (70) is not quasi-exhaustive in major terms, because it can be replaced by an equivalence. Yet we can add the converse implication, which is not derivable from (70), and thus construct a semi-admissible conjunction such that (70) is quasi-exhaustive in major terms except for this conjunction. Therefore (70) is supplementable and thus semi-admissible. We see that the statement about living organisms, which we would regard as a reasonable implication, possesses a formal structure which allows for this classification.

We could also add (70a) to (70) and thus make it quasi-exhaustive in elementary terms. But this is not always possible. Consider, for instance, (69) and assume that not only (68), but also the relation

(71) $$b \supset a . c$$

holds. Then (69) is no longer quasi-exhaustive in major terms. But it is still supplementable and thus semi-admissible, because we can add (71) and thus arrive at a semi-admissible conjunction such that (69) is quasi-exhaustive in major terms except for this conjunction. However, we cannot make it quasi-exhaustive in elementary terms. When we also add (68), in order to include the restrictive condition for elementary terms, we see that in this conjunction (69) is redundant, because it is derivable from (68). For this reason, we do not require in definition 34 that it be possible to make the statement p a factor in a conjunction such that p is quasi-exhaustive in elementary terms except for this conjunction; we only require that this can be done for major terms.

Finally, assume that we have an implication of the second order

(72) $$a \supset b$$

in which the implicans is false of second order. Here the terms abbreviated by 'a' and 'b' may, or may not, be composed of elementary terms. Now (72) is not quasi-exhaustive in major terms, though it still is reduced. But when we add the condition '$\bar{a}$', or some equivalent of it, we can cancel, in the resulting conjunction, the implicate of (72); in other words, within this conjunction, (72) is not reduced. Therefore (72) cannot be made, without a change, a factor in a reduced conjunction as required in definition 34, and is thus not supplementable and not semi-admissible (requirement 1.10*). The same consideration applies if the implicate of (72) is true of second order. We see that requirement 1.10* rules out implications of second order if their implicans is false of an order $\geqq 2$, and likewise if their implicate is true of an order $\geqq 2$. However, it admits implications which can be replaced by equivalences. Finally, second-order implications of the form '$a \supset b.c$', in which 'c' is true of second order, are ruled out by requirement 1.8*. The same holds for second-order implications of the form '$a \vee b \supset c$' in which 'c' is false of second order.

Similar considerations can easily be carried through for the other operations, and we have the theorem analogous to theorem 11:

Theorem 13. If a statement is semi-admissible, the only cases where the statement can be non-quasi-exhaustive in major terms are the following ones: the statement may be an implication which can be replaced by an equivalence, or it may be an inclusive disjunction which can be replaced by an exclusive one.

For these reasons, semi-admissible statements can be accepted as reasonable. They either include the condition restricting their major T-cases, or this condition can be added without changing the statement. In the latter case, the semi-admissible statement appears reasonable *within a certain context*; the restrictive condition for the major T-cases may be kept in the background, so to speak, ready to be added, while we know that this addition can be done without cutting down the statement. Reasonableness appears here as a *wholeness property*; a statement taken alone is in this case not reasonable, but is so if it can be made a part of a reasonable whole. This kind of reasonableness is explicated by the term *semi-admissible*. There are many illustrations for this kind of statement. For instance, we say: 'if a number is divisible by 10, it is divisible by 2 and 5', although the grammatical conjunction 'if and only if' would be more appropriate. Or we say: 'if a body gets warmer, its molecules are speeded up'. We would regard this implication as reasonable, because we think of the tacit addition: 'and if the molecules of the body are speeded up, it gets warmer'. Again, an 'if and only if' would be more appropriate; it would raise the statement from semi-admissible to fully admissible status.

With these implications, we have finally admitted the synthetic forms ruled out previously, where implicans and implicate are elementary terms and the converse implication is synthetic nomological. For instance, we may very well consider the terms 'magnetic north pole' and 'magnetic south pole' as elementary terms; nonetheless, the statement 'if the earth has a magnetic north pole, it also has a magnetic southpole' is accepted as semi-admissible, although its converse implication is likewise nomological and is not derivable from it. It is derivable only when we add the corresponding law of nature concerning magnetism. With the addition of the category of semi-admissible statements, we thus have admitted all forms of implications that can be replaced by equivalences.

Since fully admissible statements include both original nomological statements and those statements which are fully admissible by derivation, whereas semi-admissible statements do not include fully admissible statements, we define admissible statements as their joint class:

Definition 36. A statement is *admissible* if it is either fully admissible or semi-admissible. The major operation of an admissible statement is called an admissible operation. (*V*-term.)

The classification of nomological statements introduced by definitions 27, 28, 29, 33, 35, 36, is represented in the following table. The categories named inside the rectangles drawn in the diagram do not overlap with other categories; the overlapping categories are named outside. The nonoverlapping categories are defined by positive requirements and the addition of negative requirements stating that a previous category is excluded. However, every category satisfies the positive requirements of every nonoverlapping category to the right of it.

We shall now derive some theorems for admissible statements in general. We see from definition 35 that a factor of a semi-admissible

TABLE OF NOMOLOGICAL STATEMENTS

nomological and true of second order

admissible

fully admissible

	original nomological	fully admissible by derivation	semi-admissible	merely nomological
analytic synthetic				
			no statements in this category	

admissible

nomological and true of third order

conjunction is at least semi-admissible. Combining this result with theorem 12, we derive the theorem:

Theorem 14. If a conjunction is admissible, its factors are admissible.

Conversely, when we combine two admissible statements into a conjunction, it may happen that the conjunction is not reduced. But we can prove the theorem:

Theorem 15. A conjunction of admissible statements, possibly after reducing, is admissible.

This theorem is easily seen to be true apart from the following possibility. In the reducing process one of the statements may be so changed that its major T-cases are not the same as before; and we have to show that the statement remains, at least, supplementable. This is shown as follows.

Assume that the statement p, which is to be included in the conjunction, is of second order and that in the reducing process it has been changed into p'. Let the major operation of p be a disjunction. It is impossible that one of the major terms of p is canceled in the reducing process, because then we could derive the truth of the other major term from the conjunction, and this term would thus be true of the same order as p. Therefore, p' is a disjunction whose major terms result from canceling units within the major terms of p. If the canceled units were connected to the remaining part of the term by an 'or', none of the major terms of p' can be true of second order or higher, because then it would have been so before the canceling. If the canceled units were connected to the remaining part of the term by an 'and', none of the major terms of p' can be true of second order, either, because of requirement 1.7*. The same result follows from 1.8* if the equivalence was the connecting relation. Therefore, p' is still supplementable. A similar proof is given if the major operation of p is an implication or an equivalence. Thus theorem 15 is proved.

Turning back to the study of implications, we derive by analogy with the discussion of (51) the theorem:

Theorem 16.   If the implication

(73a) $a_1 \vee a_2 \supset b_1 . b_2$

is admissible, each of the implications

(73b) $a_i \supset b_k$ $i, k = 1,2$

is admissible; and vice versa, if the four implications (73b) are admissible of the same order, the implication (73a), possibly after reducing, is admissible.

The first part of the theorem follows directly from requirement 1.8*. The second part is easily seen to be true. If the implications (73b) are of second order, it cannot happen that the implicans of (73a) is false of second order, or that the implicate of (73a) is true of second order, because otherwise the same would happen to the relations (73b). The same inference applies if the implications are true of third order.

Let us now study contraposition in the two forms:

(74)   from '$a \supset b$'   to '$\bar{b} \supset \bar{a}$'
(75)   from '$a . c \supset b$'   to '$a . \bar{b} \supset \bar{c}$'

It is easily seen that, for synthetic statements, these transitions have no influence upon the satisfaction of requirements 2.1–2.2 and 1.6–1.9. Thus we have the theorem:

Theorem 17.   If the contraposition (74) or (75) is applied to a synthetic fully admissible implication, the resulting implication, possibly after canceling double negation lines, is fully admissible.

However, we can make this inference for semi-admissible implications only with respect to the transition (74), because here the major T-cases are the same before and after the transition. For the transition (75), this is not the case. Consider, for instance, the example (69). If we apply to it contraposition according to (75), the resulting implicans is false of second order, and the implication is thus not supplementable and not semi-admissible. Using the illustration given for (69), we would have here the implication: 'if a metal is heated and does not expand, it is not red', which is certainly unreasonable. We see that the concept *semi-admissible* takes account of this fact and characterizes a category of implications which require precaution as to contraposition. We have the theorem:

Theorem 18. If the contraposition (74) is applied to a semi-admissible implication, the resulting implication, possibly after canceling double negation lines, is semi-admissible. But if the contraposition (75) is applied to a semi-admissible implication, the resulting implication may not be semi-admissible.

For admissible tautologies, contraposition is likewise restricted to the form (74); the form (75) may lead to non-admissible tautologies, as is shown by the tautology '$a.b \supset a$', which is admissible, whereas its contrapositive '$a.\bar{a} \supset b$' is nonreduced and nonadmissible.

Some further theorems concerning implications will now be studied. With respect to transitivity we have the following theorem:

Theorem 19. If the implications

(76a) $a \supset b$ $b \supset c$ (76b)

are admissible of the same order, then the implication

(76c) $a \supset c$

possibly after reducing, is admissible.

That reducing may be necessary is seen when we put '$a.c$' for 'c'. The proof of the theorem is given as follows.

Let us first assume that (76a–b) are both true of second order; then (76c), being derivable from the two statements, is true of at least second order. Thus requirement 2.1 is satisfied. Furthermore, requirement 1.10* is satisfied when neither 'a' is false of second order nor 'c' true of second order; but this must be the case, because otherwise 1.10* would be violated by one of the relations (76a–b). We now must study requirement 1.8*. If it were violated by (76c), we could write the latter relation in the form

$$(77a) \qquad a_1 \vee a_2 \supset c_1 . c_2$$

such that each side, taken separately, is reduced, whereas

$$(77b) \qquad a_1 \supset c_1$$

is not reduced or not supplementable. In the latter case, either 'a_1' is false of second or higher order, or 'c_1' is true of second or higher order. But then one of the relations (76a–b) violates 1.8*. So there remains only the possibility that (77b) is not reduced. If reducing this relation leads to either '$\bar{a}_1$' or 'c_1', we have the same case as before and thus conclude that this cannot occur. Therefore, reducing can only concern the inner structure of one of the terms of (77b). But if some unit within these terms can be canceled, the same can be done within (77a), and therefore, as is easily seen, also within (76c). Now the latter form was assumed to be reduced. This proves theorem 19 for the case that (76a–b) are true of second order. A similar proof is given if these two statements are true of third order.

If relations (76a–b) are true of different orders, exceptions to theorem 19 can arise. For instance, (76a) may be true of second order, while (76b) is true of third order and 'c' is true of second order. Then (76c) is not admissible, because it is true of second order and its implicate is true of the same order. Here 'b' cannot be true of higher than first order, because (76a) is true of second order. But 'b' can also be false of first or second order. Such cases cannot be excluded by the theory.

It is not possible to derive theorem 19 with respect to fully admissible implications alone. If (76a–b) are fully admissible, it may happen that (76c) is merely semi-admissible. Consider, for instance, the implications

$$(78a) \quad a \supset b \qquad\qquad\qquad b \supset c_1 \vee c_2 \quad (78b)$$

which we will assume fully admissible of second order. The derivable implication

(78c) $$a \supset c_1 \vee c_2$$

need not be fully admissible. If '$a \supset \bar{c}_2$' is true of second order, and (78c) is true of second order, (78c) is not quasi-exhaustive in elementary terms. An illustration is given by the following sentences:

(79)

> When the telephone rings, I go to the telephone.
> When I go to the telephone, I turn the dial or
> I answer the call.
> ———————————————————
> When the telephone rings, I turn the dial or I
> answer the call.

The conclusion is merely semi-admissible and appears not quite reasonable because, when the telephone rings, I do not turn the dial. It is not quasi-exhaustive in elementary terms.

We go on with the study of implications. When an implication

(80) $$a \supset b$$

is admissible of the order k, the implication

(81) $$a.c \supset b$$

is certainly nomological, being derivable from (80). Now (81) may be admissible, as is seen from the illustration given for (69), where this form is semi-admissible. But (81) *need not* be admissible, because the conjunction '$a.c$' may be false of an order $\geq k$. For instance, let (80) be the second-order implication, 'when an ice cube is heated, it contracts'. For (81) we put the implication, 'when an ice cube of 86° is heated, it contracts'. Since a physical law excludes the existence of an ice cube at 86°, the implicans is here false of the same order as the implication is true, and this implication is therefore not admissible.

The rule leading from (80) to (81) may be called the *invariance principle* of implication. We see that this principle, though indispensable for all forms of logical implication, does not hold for admissible implications. The reason is that the latter are dependent, not only on truth conditions, but also on conditions for the form of writing.

That the implication (81) must be excluded, in the example considered, from admissible statements is shown by the following consideration. We know the physical law that water of 86° when heated, expands, which can be written as

$$(82) \qquad\qquad c \supset \bar{b}$$

and we thus derive the second-order implication

$$(83) \qquad\qquad a.c \supset \bar{b}$$

In words this means, 'if an ice cube of 86° is heated, it expands'. Since (83) is as good as (81), these implications cannot be used for the expression of a conditional contrary to fact, because they state, for the case that the implicans were true, contradictory consequences.

Implications of the form

$$(84a) \quad a \supset b \qquad\qquad\qquad\qquad a \supset \bar{b} \quad (84b)$$

may be called *contrary implications*. If they are true of the order k, we derive that their implicans 'a' is false of the order k; therefore neither of them is admissible.

Theorem 20. If two contrary implications are true of the same order, neither one is admissible.

This result does not apply, however, to contrary implications of different orders. The implicans is then false of the lower order and the higher-order implication can be admissible. Referring to the above example concerning a man touching a high-voltage wire, we find that the contrary implication, according to which he would not have been killed if there had been current in the wire, is inadmissible because it is true merely of first order, while the implicans is false of the same order. Similar results hold for higher-order implications. For instance, the statement 'an ice cube of 86° is not spherically shaped' appears reasonable. This implication is of third order, while its implicans is false of second order, and thus it is quasi-exhaustive and admissible.

Obviously, the lower-order implication can then not be admissible, because its implicans is false of the same order. For instance, the implication 'an ice cube of 86° is spherically sphaped'', though true of second order, is not admissible. We have the theorem:

Theorem 21. Two contrary implications cannot be both admissible.

To have another example, consider the statement, 'if a signal travels faster than light, it arrives at a distant point earlier than a light ray departing simultaneously with it'. This statement, too, is admissible, because it is true of third order, while its implicans is false of second order. The contrary implication, stating that the signal would arrive later than the light ray, is true of second order and thus inadmissible. This example shows that, in the theory here presented, we can state in an admissible form tautological implications of assumptions that are ruled out by physical laws. But we cannot admissibly state synthetic implications of such assumptions. In fact, only implications of the first kind are regarded as reasonable in the practice of the scientist. In order to compare an accepted theory with a non-accepted one, the physicist often computes mathematical consequences of the non-accepted theory, and regards his results as reasonable conditionals contrary to fact.

With this solution of the problem of contrary implications, my present theory appears superior to my previous theory, which could exclude contrary implications only for the case that the implicans was false of first order. I used there [1] a 'qualification of derivation' in order to define a reasonable implication; an implication was accepted as reasonable if it was derivable from a set s of original nomological statements from which the falsehood of its implicans was not derivable. Although this rule appears plausible at first sight, it can be shown that it cannot rule out contrary implications whose implicans is false of the same order as the implication is true. Assume that the above implication (80) is derivable from a set s_1 of original nomological statements; then (81) is derivable from the same set s_1. Assume, furthermore, that the implication (82) is derivable from a different set s_2 of original nomological statements, which, however, is true of the same order as s_1; then (83) is also derivable from s_2. Each of the implications

---

[1] ESL, p. 370–371. When we replace in the example (20) given there the last words by '...implies x sinks down', the resulting contrary implication would also satisfy the qualification of derivation, and would thus be accepted by the older theory as nomological in the narrower sense.

(81) and (83) is thus derivable from a set of original nomological statements from which the falsehood of the implicans is not derivable, and hence each of these two contrary implications is accepted. Their implicans, of course, is false of the same order as the implications are true.

This consideration shows that the mentioned qualification of derivation is inappropriate to supply conditionals contrary to fact which are safe from including contrary implications. If it appears desirable to introduce synthetic counterfactuals whose implicans contradicts a physical law, one would have to proceed otherwise. It may be feasible to define a subdivision of synthetic nomological statements in such a way that a further stratification of orders of truth is constructed. Such a procedure, for which I see at present no specific need, would once more represent a theory of reasonable implications in terms of orders of truth. For these reasons it appears that an order-theory of truth is indispensable to solve the problem of conditionals contrary to fact.

The inability to understand conditionals contrary to fact is often regarded as evidence for a low capacity of abstraction in children and primitive people. There is a story told about a South American Indian who, in a class on arithmetic given by a missionary, was unable to answer the question: if a white man shoots 6 bears in one day, how many bears would he shoot in 5 days? On further inquiry, the missionary finally received the answer: a white man cannot shoot 6 bears in one day. It is an interesting fact that, on certain conditions, the theory of conditionals contrary to fact leads back to the attitude of the primitive man who rejects a nomological implication because the implicans is impossible; this is the case if the implicans is false of the same order as the implication is true. The correct reply to the Indian who had his doubts about a white man's ability of hunting would have been: according to your views, the implicans is false of second order; but the question concerns a statement of third order and is therefore meaningful. I doubt, however, whether the missionary's capacity for abstraction would have been high enough to understand this answer.

VI

EXTENSION OF VERIFIABILITY

After the definition of nomological statements in the wider and in the narrower sense, a certain extension of the definitions must now be considered.

The use of admissible statements is not always sufficient for the practice of science. In order to discuss scientific theories, we sometimes use procedures in which empirical truth is deliberately disregarded. For instance, we may dispense with some established laws and consider the system of the remaining laws; or we may even replace established laws by contradictory ones and consider the resulting system S, though this system is known to be false. The theory of nomological statements is then applicable with the following changes. Instead of the term 'verifiably true' we use the term 'accepted for S'; and the term 'admissible' is replaced by the term 'admissible in S'. Within the system S, certain statements will then appear as reasonable which are considered unreasonable within the system S_0, which is based on the concept 'verifiably true'.

For instance, we can construct a theory of time without using Einstein's law that light is the fastest signal, but keeping to the synthetic law that if a signal makes a round trip, its arrival is later than its departure (which excludes infinite velocities for signals). In such a system, the statement 'if a signal travels faster than light, and makes a round trip, its arrival is later than its departure', is admissible, although in the system S_0 it is inadmissible, being true of second order, while the implicans is false of second order. Or we can make the fictitious assumption that there were negative as well as positive masses, whose mutual attraction follows rules analogous to those holding for the attraction of electric charges; then we could derive the statement, 'of any three masses, at least two repel each other'. This would be an admissible statement in this system, although it is false in S_0.

This shows that the theory of nomological statements can be

carried through for any system S which supplies a sufficient substitute for the concept 'verifiably true'. The theory of the system S_0 is included among these theories; it is the one that applies to actual science.

I will now show that a concept *verifiably true in the wider sense* can be defined, which makes it permissible to say that there may be laws of nature which will never by found by human beings.

Beginning with the system S_0, we define modalities as explained in ESL, § 65. The term *physically possible* then refers to any occurrence not excluded by a nomological statement, i.e., not excluded by a statement of S_0. An occurrence denoted by q *is physically possible relative to the occurrence denoted by p* if neither q nor $\bar{q}$ is deductively derivable from p by the use of the class S_0 (ESL, p. 396).

Furthermore, the system S_0 leads to definitions of kinds of physical objects and quantities, such as temperature, voltage, wave length, etc.; but also including such things as trees, planets, human beings, cats, etc. For the observation of such objects we have developed *observational procedures*. For instance, looking at a cat is an observational procedure to ascertain the color of its skin, but unsuitable to ascertain the content of its stomach; directing a telescope to the night sky is an observational procedure suitable for the observation of stars, but unsuitable for the observation of radio waves. The result of an observational procedure is an *observational datum*. There are actual and possible observational data; for instance, the temperature of a certain room during a certain night is an actual or a possible observational datum, depending on whether observations by means of a thermometer were made.

Speaking of possible data has the following meaning. Using actual data and known laws of nature, we can derive the implication: 'if at the time t and the place x a certain known observational procedure had been used, a datum of a certain kind would have been observed'. This implication is nomological relative to the actual data on which it is based, and thus derivable from these data in terms of S_0. Usually, the implication does not tell us the specific value of the datum, but only the kind to which the datum belongs. For instance, we can say that using a thermometer a certain temperature would have been observed, but we do not know which. Sometimes we can even derive the specific value; for instance, we can say, 'if ancient astronomers had used telescopes, they would have seen the moons of Jupiter'.

With the discovery of new laws, new observational procedures are constructed. For instance, the discovery of the photo-electric effect led to using photographic films as observational instruments. Futhermore, new laws are sometimes discovered by extending the range of known observational procedures. Before 1896, it had not been known that wrapping a photographic plate in opaque paper and putting a piece of ore on top of it, is a method producing a blackening of the emulsion (after development); in the year mentioned, Becquerel thus discovered the radiation of uranium ore. This discovery was due to chance; no one had anticipated that the range of the observational possibilities contained in a photographic emulsion could thus be extended. Extending the range of an observational procedure means, logically speaking, using the procedure even when we have no implication stating that a datum of a certain new kind will be observed, but merely know that at least a datum of a known kind will occur, though perhaps a trivial one. Becquerel knew, of course, that putting the ore on the wrapped plate must lead to some observation; he expected it would lead to a state of the plate which, on developing, would show no blackening. When we speak of possible data, we shall include the use of observational procedures in an extended range.

The if-statements I am making here are conditionals contrary to fact; but they presuppose merely nomological statements contained in S_0. This is clear because the implications do not state the specific value of the observation; they merely refer to '*the* result of the observation', and that there will be some definite result follows from laws contained in S_0. This shows, however, that a merely possible datum is not determined by R_0, P_0, S_0, but depends on the nature of the physical world. The combination R_0, P_0, S_0, determines definite descriptions, and a datum is given by a statement assigning some further property to the description, such as, 'the result of the observational procedure is a black spot'. This statement is synthetic and usually cannot be asserted without actual observation. In other words, we may say that the combination R_0, P_0, S_0, determines the observational questions we can ask; the answer is given by physical reality. For this reason, I shall regard the class R_1 as a well-defined class, although we do not know, and never shall know, all the observational data belonging to R_1.

Given the class R_1, I shall regard it as permissible to speak of the class S_1 of nomological statements verifiable on the basis R_1. The latter term means that it is logically possible to verify these statements inductively on the observational basis R_1. The class S_1 is thus defined just like the class S_0, using requirements 1.1–1.10 and definitions 27–28, with the qualification, however, that the term 'verifiably true' is replaced by the term 'verifiable on the basis R_1'. The class S_1 may be regarded as supplying the explicans of the term 'all existing laws of nature' in contradistinction to the term 'all laws of nature known at some time', which is explicated by means of S_0. The class S_1 might include, for instance, laws of a certain kind of radiation which forever has escaped, and will escape, the observations of our physicists. And the term 'verifiable on the basis R_1' may be considered as the explicans of the term 'verifiably true in the wider sense'.

If the class S_1 appears not comprehensive enough, an iteration of the definition may be employed. We can speak of the class P_1 of observational procedures which it is logically possible to construct for S_1 and R_1, and then define in terms of R_1, P_1, S_1, a class R_2 of possible observational data and a class S_2 of nomological statements, repeating the form of definition used before. This iteration may be continued. Are we allowed to speak of the joint class S_∞ (union) of all the classes S_1, S_2, ...? This is presumably permissible. However this may be, the statement 's is a law of nature' may be interpreted as meaning, 'in the series S_1, S_2, ... there is an S_i which includes s'. And the term 'verifiably true in the wider sense' may then be interpreted as meaning, 'there is a basis R_i on which it is logically possible to verify the statement'. For all practical purposes, the class S_1 is a sufficient approximation to the concept 'all existing laws of nature'; and the concept 'verifiable on the basis R_1', to the concept 'verifiably true in the wider sense'.

VII

COUNTERFACTUALS OF NONINTERFERENCE

The conditionals contrary to fact so far considered, also called *regular conditionals contrary to fact*, are used when 'a' is false and 'b' is false, and we assert that if 'a' were true, 'b' would be true. There is a second kind of conditional contrary to fact. It is used when 'a' is false and 'b' is true; we then assert that if 'a' had been true, 'b' would still be true. Statements of this kind, which we will call *counterfactuals of noninterference*, must now be investigated.

It is a sufficient condition for this kind of counterfactual assertion that '$a \supset b$' be admissible. Obviously, this presupposes that '$\bar{a} \supset b$' is not true of the same order, because otherwise 'b' would also be true of this order, and neither one of the two implications would be admissible. Calling such statements *implications with contrary antecedents*, we have the following theorem:

Theorem 22. If an implication is admissible, the implication with contrary antecedent is not admissible.

But statements of this kind are rather trivial if they depend on the admissibility of '$a \supset b$'. For instance, if an airplane arrives safely and one of the passengers has died of heart failure on the trip, we may say, 'if the plane had crashed into the mountains, the man would also be dead'. We are usually not interested in this trivial implication; we wish to assert such counterfactual implications as, 'if the plane had had a different pilot, the passenger would also be dead'. In an implication of this form, we do not assert that 'a' implies 'b' in a connective implication, or that 'a' entails 'b', but merely that 'a' does not interfere with 'b'.

It can be shown that these counterfactuals of noninterference allow for a rather simple treatment, which does not presuppose the theory of admissible implications but can be given completely within the frame of the theory of probability.

For this investigation we have to introduce probability expressions concerning statements 'a' and 'b'. Since probabilities refer to classes, whereas the present theory concerns statements, there exists a certain ambiguity in finding for these statements suitable classes which afford the possibility of constructing meaningful probability values for the statements. It will be assumed that this construction can be carried out. [1] In particular, a suitable reference class has to be constructed which refers to the general situation G in which the statement 'b' has been verified and which confers a degree of probability on 'b'. This general reference class G will be omitted in the formulae; we thus use the absolute notation [2] and write probability expressions in the form '$P(b)$', '$P(a, b)$'. Since these probabilities, in a transfer of meaning, refer to single cases, they can be regarded as *weights*. We will always assume that these probabilities are *genuine* (see the appendix, definition VI).

Using these considerations concerning reference classes for the assignment of weights to individual statements, we now proceed to define noninterference.

Definition 37. A statement 'a' does not interfere with a statement 'b' if and only if

(87) $$P(a, b) \geq P(b)$$

If the equality sign holds, 'a' is irrelevant to 'b'; otherwise it is positively relevant. Noninterference is thus defined as the absence of negative relevance. For instance, if we have reasons to believe that a certain person is intelligent (statement 'b'), it will be irrelevant of we get the further information (statement 'a') that he is 20 years old. Furthermore, the information that he is a trained mathematician will be positively relevant and thus does not interfere with statement 'b', whereas the information that he repeatedly failed in academic examinations would be negatively relevant and would thus interfere with 'b'. To give another illustration, imagine that a tennis player who is not in good form wins a match. We then would say: if he had been in better form, he would also have won (positive relevance). But we would say, likewise: if there had

---

[1] I refer to the discussion in ThP. For the problem of the reference class see p. 47 and p. 374. The term 'weight' is there discussed on p. 378 and p. 408. The notation of this book is used for the following presentation.

[2] ThP, p. 106.

been more spectators, he would also have won (irrelevance).
Using the theorem of the calculus of probability: [1]

(88) $$\frac{P(a,b)}{P(b,a)} = \frac{P(b)}{P(a)}$$

we derive from (87)

(89) $$P(b, a) \geqq P(a)$$

Noninterference is thus a symmetrical relationship: if 'a' does not
interfere with 'b', then 'b' does not interfere with 'a'.

We now introduce the following definition:

Definition 38. If 'b' is true and 'a' is false, then the counterfactual of noninterference, 'if 'a' had been true, 'b' would also be
true', is *permissible* if relation (87) is satisfied.

We use here the term 'permissible' because the counterfactual
considered need not be an admissible statement; in fact, it need
not even be a nomological statement and can be a first-order
statement. The class of reasonable conditionals contrary to fact is
thus somewhat wider than the class of admissible implications;
this result will be confirmed by the investigations of the following
chapter and will be formulated in definition 42.

We must now explain why the counterfactual of noninterference
is permissible on these rather simple conditions, whereas the
regular conditional contrary to fact, or counterfactual of interference, requires the involved theory of admissible statements.

Assume we know that the probability $P(a, b)$ is very high, and
that it satisfies the conditions of a genuine probability. We would
then be willing to use it for predictions; if 'a' has been observed,
we shall predict 'b'. Would we also use it for a regular conditional
contrary to fact? Assuming that neither 'a' nor 'b' are true, would
we be willing to say, 'if 'a' had been true, 'b' would have been true'?
I think we would hesitate to do so; since a high probability admits
of exceptions, we might argue that this particular instance might
have been a case of exception. Why do we thus distinguish between
a predictive and a counterfactual usage?

The predictive use of high probabilities is justified by the

---

[1] ThP, p. 112, formula (32).

frequency interpretation when we regard predictions as posits; our posits will then be true in a high percentage of cases. In the same way we could argue that regular counterfactuals of high probabilities could be asserted as posits and then would be true in a high percentage of cases. Although the latter conclusion appears correct, there is an important difference between these two kinds of posits. For a predictive use, we can verify the individual posit later, by waiting until observation tells us whether the posit was true. For counterfactual use, no such individual verification is possible; in fact, although we know that the majority of our counterfactual posits would be true, we would never know which of them are true, i.e., which of them are members of this majority. For this reason, we hesitate to apply the counterfactual in an individual case. We would prefer to use counterfactuals only when there is evidence that they are not subject to exceptions. It is this very condition which is satisfied for nomological statements, or laws of nature; and for this reason, we restrict regular conditionals contrary to fact to admissible statements as defined in the preceding chapters.

Now it can be shown that for counterfactuals of the noninterference kind this difficulty can be circumvented in a certain way. Although, of course, such conditionals contrary to fact cannot be verified individually either, it turns out that there is no objection to assuming that they are always true, without exceptions. This is seen as follows.

Assume that we have a certain series of event, for which 'b' is sometimes true, and a parallel series containing 'a':

$$(90) \qquad \begin{array}{l} .\,.\,a\,a\,.\,a\,.\,.\,.\,.\,.\,. \\ b\,\,b\,\,b\,\,\bar{b}\,\,\bar{b}\,\,b\,\,\bar{b}\,\,b\,\,b\,\,.\,.\,. \end{array}$$

For the cases where 'a' is false we have put a dot. We will assume that $P(a, b) < 1$, although it may be a high value; then there will be cases where an 'a' is accompanied by a '$\bar{b}$'. We will also assume that the probabilities $P(a)$ and $P(b)$ exist. The question arises: if there were more cases 'a', i.e., if $P(a)$ were higher, can we arrange the cases 'a' in such a way that every 'b' is accompanied by an 'a' without changing the values $P(b)$ and $P(a, b)$? In other words:

can we replace every dot above a '*b*' by an '*a*', and then by replacing some, or all, of the remaining dots likewise by cases '*a*' arrive at a distribution such that the percentage of cases '*a*' accompanied by '*b*' among all cases '*a*' is the same as the previous percentage?

In probability terms this means: can we add the condition '$b \supset a$', or its statistical substitute $P(b, a) = 1$, to given values of $P(b)$ and $P(a, b)$? The answer follows from relation (88). If we put there $P(b, a) = 1$, we infer, because $P(a) \leqq 1$, that the resulting left-hand side $P(a, b)$ is greater than or equal to the value $P(b)$ on the right-hand side and thus that the inequality (87) must hold. In other words, relation (87) formulates the condition which the given probabilities $P(b)$ and $P(a, b)$ must satisfy in order that it be possible to put an '*a*' above every '*b*' in (90). It was explained that we then shall also have to put some cases '*a*' above cases '$\bar{b}$' in order to keep the given probablities unchanged; but we can thus at least satisfy the conditon '$b \supset a$'.

This means: if condition (87) is satisfied, it is permissible to assume that, if there were more cases '*a*', every case '*b*' would be accompanied by an '*a*'. This assumption would not contradict the observed statistical values of $P(b)$ and $P(a, b)$. Since our counter-factual merely states that the occurrence of '*b*' would not be in-validated if '*a*' had come true, we conclude that we are allowed to say: if only there had been more cases '*a*', all our counterfactuals would have been true. This assumption is permissible although $P(a, b) < 1$.

Note that we do not have a proof that all the counterfactuals would have been true. Such a proof is of course impossible. What we can prove is merely that we have no proof to the contrary, i.e., that the statement: 'all our counterfactuals would have been true if there had been more cases '*a*'', is a permissible addition to our system of assertions, an addition which does not lead to contra-dictions. This addition may be regarded as an extension rule of our language,[1] a convention, which allows us to speak of the truth of conditionals contrary to fact; and we can prove that it is a permissible extension rule. This consideration justifies definition

---

[1]   See my book *The Rise of Scientific Philosophy*, Berkeley 1951, p. 267.

38 and with it the incorporation of counterfactuals of noninterference into permissible statements.

A similar proof cannot be given for conditionals contrary to fact of the regular kind, which assert interference. If $P(a, b) < 1$, and we assert that if 'a' had been true, 'b' would have been true, this conditional contrary to fact cannot be true in all cases; i.e., the statement: 'if there had been more cases 'a', all these counterfactuals would have been true', is certainly false. This means that for counterfactuals of interference an extension rule corresponding to the given one would be impermissible. This is the reason that such conditionals contrary to fact require a specific treatment by the help of admissible statements, which restrict the use of such conditionals contrary to fact to implications which we may regard as true without exceptions.

VIII

RELATIVE NOMOLOGICAL STATEMENTS

In conversational and in scientific language we often use statements q which are not nomological, but which are nomologically derivable from some matter of fact, i.e., from a statement p which is true of first order. A statement q of this kind is itself true of first order, because otherwise we would not need the statement p to derive q. However, there must be some nomological statement s, or a set of such statements, such that q is deductively derivable from $p.s$. Since then $p.s \supset q$ is tautological, and this is the same as $s \supset (p \supset q)$, the statement $p \supset q$ is derivable from s, and is thus nomological. We therefore introduce the following definition, in which we assume p and q to be separate closed units, or else to be statements having no variables:

Definition 39. If p and q are true of first order, then q is nomological relative to p if $p \supset q$ is nomological.

This category of statements [1] has many practical applications. For instance, we call it a law of nature that the earth moves on an elliptic orbit around the sun. More precisely speaking, this is a relative nomological statement. It is derivable from the law of gravitation, if certain initial conditions for the relative position and velocity of earth and sun are assumed. Since such conditions do actually hold, the statement is nomological relative to these conditions. Often the conditions are not explicitly stated, but regarded as understood, and then the relative nomological statement is treated like an absolute one. Note that these statements differ from semi-admissible statements, because they are merely true of first order, whereas the latter are nomological. When we say that

---

[1] Relative nomological statements were introduced in ESL, § 63. This section of ESL is to be replaced by the present chapter. Relative modalities were defined in ESL, § 65, by the use of relative nomological statements; this section of ESL remains unchanged.

a statement q is relative-nomological of the order k, we refer the order k, not to the relative statement q (which is of first order) but to the statement $p \supset q$.

With the definition of relative nomological statements we have constructed statements in which certain secondary operations can be regarded as reasonable. In order to satisfy the stronger requirements of reasonableness, comparable to those laid down for admissible statements, we will now define a narrower class, to be called relative admissible statements. We use the following definition, in which again the statements p and q may possess operators, but must be closed units:

Definition 40. If p and q are true of first order, then q is *admissible relative* to p if $p \supset q$ is admissible. (V-term).

The use of relative admissible statements is particularly important if the relative statement is itself an implication '$b \supset c$'. We then have two implications in series, putting 'a' for p:

(91) $a \supset (b \supset c)$

If '$b \supset c$' represents an admissible statement relative to 'a', we have here a case where not only the major implication, but also a following secondary implication is reasonable.

However, even if the total statement is admissible, a secondary implication is not unconditionally reasonable, like a primary one. It is subject to certain restrictions when used for a conditional contrary to fact. Let (91) be admissible, and let us assume that we know that 'a' is true and 'b' is false. Can we then reasonably assert that the truth of 'b' would have implied the truth of 'c'? There are two ways of formulating this counterfactual conditional:

1)   If 'b' had been true and 'a' had remained true, then 'c' would have been true.

2)   If 'b' had been true, then 'c' would have been true.

The first formulation is obviously justified as much as the counterfactual conditional of any other admissible implication. It uses (91) in the form

(92) $a.b \supset c$

in which the implication directed to 'c' is moved into the major place; it therefore is completely dealt with in the previous theory.

It is different with the second formulation, which refers to the secondary implication taken alone and may be called a *secondary conditional contrary to fact*, to be distinguished from the *primary conditional contrary to fact* of formulation 1. Obviously, formulation 2 is true only if we add another conditional contrary to fact and have reason to regard it as true:

3) If '*b*' had been true, '*a*' would also have been true. On what condition are we entitled to make this assertion?

In order to answer this question, we have to examine more carefully what we mean when we say that the premise '*a*' is omitted, although in some sense it is still referred to. Let us call '*a*' the *major antecedent*, and '*b*' the *minor antecedent*, of the *serial implication* (91); the statement '*c*' may be called, as usual, the *consequent*. We can now distinguish two different interpretations of the act of omitting the major antecedent.

First, we can say that the relative implication asserted separately is regarded as true only on the assumption that the major antecedent is true. The use of the relative implication in separate form then merely represents an elliptic mode of speech i.e., formulation 2 is then elliptic for formulation 1. In this interpretation, formulation 2 offers no problems, because statement 3 is then trivially satisfied, being elliptic for '$a.b \supset a$'.

It appears, however, that in actual usage we do not regard statement 3 as a trivial tautology, but wish to express in this statement a certain hypothesis; in other words, that we regard it as a permissible conditional contrary to fact, though of the non-interference kind studied in chapter 7. This consideration leads to a second interpretation of relative implications. There is still some premise regarded as understood; but this premise is not statement '*a*' itself. We think, rather, of the general situation *G* which causally produces the event referred to in '*a*', a situation which we have good reason to assume as existing and which confers upon '*a*' a high degree of probability, although its description does not directly include '*a*'. Only on this interpretation will statement 3 represent an empirical hypothesis.

That this interpretation corresponds to the usage of language is seen from illustrations in which we question the truth of statement

3. Assume that we regard the following statement as true: If Peter comes to the party, then if Paul comes we shall have a heated discussion on religious subjects. Suppose that Peter came, but Paul did not come. Can we now say: if Paul had come, we would have witnessed a heated controversy on religious subjects? Perhaps we know that Peter has been annoyed by similar discussions with Paul; then we might argue, assuming that Peter would have known about Paul's intention to come: if Paul had come, Peter would not have come. And we would then refuse to assert the relative implication separately. This rejection of the conditional contrary to fact expressed in statement 3 indicates that statement 'a' cannot be regarded as the inarticulate premise of the relative implication asserted separately.

We shall accept this second interpretation of relative implications for the following investigation. The usage of language is often vague; but this interpretation seems more adequate than the first, because it can account for cases in which we regard the relative implication as false if it is taken separately. And we shall assume that within a given context it is sufficiently clear what general situation G is tacitly presupposed with the use of relative implications. In the example of Peter's coming, for instance, the situation G may include the fact that Peter was invited to the party, that he usually accepts such invitations, that he would know whether Paul would come, etc. In other examples G may include all kinds of evidence we have for 'a'. For instance, when we say, 'if a plane flies due west all the time, it will return to its starting point', the situation G will include the observational evidence we have for the spherical shape of the earth. The statement 'the earth is a sphere' is not directly included in the description of G, because on this interpretation the relative implication would be merely elliptic for the whole serial implication.

Or consider the following example. An artillery shell destroys a house a few minutes after some soldiers left the house. We then say: if the soldiers had remained in the house a few minutes longer, they would have been killed. Here G is the situation immediately after the shell left the gun, a situation in which, due to the direction of the gun's barrel, it was very probable that the shell would hit the house. For this situation, the relative implication can be asserted, because the fact that there are soldiers in the house is irrelevant to the path of the shell. Although a direct hit of the house may be rather improbable in general, i.e., if the total period of shooting is used as reference class, such a hit is highly probable if the situation G as described constitutes the reference class. When we change the illustration slightly, however, we might be willing to use a somewhat different reference class. Assume the shooting is part of a training program; then we might be inclined to say: if there had been soldiers in the house, the gun would not have been fired, because the command to fire would not have been given unless it was certain that there were no persons in the house. Here G is the situation immediately preceding the firing of the gun. In this situation, again, hitting the house may have been very probable if there were no soldiers in the house, because the gun may have been directly aimed at the house.

It should be noted that the necessity of the second interpretation and of the problem of finding a suitable situation G arise, not only for the use of relative implications as conditionals contrary to fact, but also for a predictive use of such implications. We often use relative implications before the truth of the major antecedent has been directly verified, if only we have sufficient evidence for its truth. For instance, when we use the example concerning the plane flying due west for a prediction, we tacitly refer to conditions, like the spherical shape of the earth, which have been verified previously and which we presume to also hold at later times; i.e., we predict the truth of the major antecedent and then assert the relative implication. This means that we use here, not a directly verified major antecedent, but merely a highly probable one. In other examples this probability may be much lower and still be good enough for predictions. For instance, we say, 'if you press the button the bell will ring'. Here we regard it as sufficiently probable that there is current in the wires, that the bell is correctly wired, etc., and do not explicitly state this assumption.

Both for predictive and counterfactual use of relative implications, therefore, we have to check whether the truth of the minor antecedent retroacts upon the truth of the major antecedent. This retroaction was illustrated above for counterfactual use. To have an illustration for predictive use, consider the statement, 'if the repair man comes the bell will ring'; this implication can scarcely be asserted, because the repair man would not have been called if the bell were in working order. It is this *retroaction* of secondary implications on their major antecedent which is the source of the difficulties and ambiguities connected with the use of such statements.

As far as a counterfactual use of relative implications is concerned, we can analyze the retroaction in terms of the theory of counterfactuals of noninterference, given in chapter 7. It is easily seen that this theory can likewise be applied to a predictive use of relative implications, since the probability considerations are of the same nature. We shall therefore now turn to construct the theory of relative implications by the help of the probability relations developed in chapter 7. We use again the absolute notation and shall not express the general reference class G in our formulae. This general reference class may be regarded as understood in all the following probability expressions.

We shall write the serial implication in the form

$$(93) \qquad a_1 \supset (a_2 \supset \overline{a_3})$$

The use of a negation line in the third term is convenient because we then can transcribe (93) into the symmetrical form

$$(94) \qquad \overline{a_1 . a_2 . a_3}$$

This form allows us to characterize serial implications by the symmetrical probability condition

$$(95) \qquad P(a_1 . a_2 . a_3) = 0$$

The theorems to be developed for relative implications are all derivable from this form. With reference to (94), we shall say that the statements 'a_1', 'a_2', 'a_3', constitute an *exclusive triplet*. If we substitute for the 'a_i' corresponding classes, relation (95) says that the common class of the three classes is empty.

The relative implications contained in (93) has the form

$$(96) \qquad a_2 \supset \overline{a_3}$$

The problem is whether this implication can be asserted separately. For this purpose we have to specify the *conditions of separability*.

The first condition concerns the major antecedent taken alone. It is to be required that in the general situation G the probability of 'a_1' is high. We thus have

(97) $$P(a_1) \sim 1$$

The curl sign means approximate equality. This requirement replaces the requirement that 'a_1' be known to be true, which we saw to be too rigid a requirement for relative implications asserted separately. The new requirement is in some sense weaker, in some other sense stronger than the requirement about the truth of 'a_1'. It is weaker in that it allows for the use of relative implications if only we have good evidence that 'a_1' is true, although 'a_1' has not been directly verified by observation; we refer to the example, 'if you press the button the bell will ring'. The reliability of the relative implication, of course, is then limited by the remaining uncertainty for 'a_1' and can only be said to be not lower than that of the assumption 'a_1'. Yet a sentence can be true although its probability is low; and in this sense, condition (97) is stronger than the requirement that 'a_1' be true. In most cases, however, an observational verification of 'a_1' is regarded as evidence for a high probability of 'a_1'; i.e., we regard the verification of 'a_1' as evidence for the existence of a situation G for which (97) is true. This means we interpret the event described by 'a_1' as the product of causal laws acting in the situation G.

For this reason, condition (97) is practically equivalent to the condition that 'a_1' be true. When we employ the secondary implication for predictions, we estimate the probability of 'a_1' and, if it is high, regard 'a_1' as true. This is illustrated by the example of the bell. When we employ the secondary implication for conditionals contrary to fact, we observe 'a_1' to be true and regard this observation as evidence for a high probability of 'a_1'; this is illustrated by the example of the shell hitting the house.

The second condition concerns the influence of the minor antecedent on the major antecedent. This condition was formulated in statement 3 for a conditional contrary to fact and then represents a counterfactual of noninterference; we shall apply it similarly for predictive use. Using relation (87) and putting there 'a_2' for 'a', 'a_1' for 'b', we formulate this condition by the inequality

$$(98) \qquad P(a_2, a_1) \geqq P(a_1)$$

If the equality sign holds, 'a_2' is irrelevant to 'a_1'. This applies to the illustration concerning an airplane flying west all the time, which occurrence is irrelevant to the statement 'a_1' that the earth is a sphere. Condition (97) is here also satisfied; thus the relative implication 'if a plane flies due west all the time, it will return to its starting point', is separable. In the example concerning Peter and Paul, (97) may be true; but we said that Paul's coming may diminish the probability of Peter's coming. Then (96) is here not separable. If we knew, in contrast, that Peter is fond of discussions on religious subjects, Paul's coming would be positively relevant to Peter's coming. Then the minor antecedent would not interfere with the major one, and the relative implication would be separable. We thus define:

Definition 41. A relative admissible implication '$a_2 \supset \overline{a_3}$' is *separable*, i.e., can be asserted by omission of its major antecedent 'a_1', if the conditions (97)–(98) of separability are satisfied.

Separable relative implications do not belong in the class of admissible statements, since they are only true of first order. We meet here with a second group of reasonable implications which are not admissible implications, to be added to the counterfactuals of noninterference. In order to include all forms of reasonable implications, we use the term 'permissible' and define:

Definition 42. An implication is *permissible* if and only if it is an admissible implication (definition 36), or a permissible counterfactual of noninterference (definition 38), or a relative admissible implication which is separable (definition 41). (*V*-term).

Note that the term 'permissible' has been defined for implications only, whereas the term 'admissible' applies to all forms of statements. We shall later extend the term 'permissible' to equivalences (definition 44).

The two relations (97)–(98) are necessary and sufficient conditions of separability. It is convenient for many purposes to replace them by the following condition, which is derivable from (97)–(98):

$$(99) \qquad\qquad P(a_2, a_1) \sim 1$$

Since (97)–(98) are not derivable from (99), relation (99) is merely a necessary, not a sufficient condition of separability.

We shall now develop the mathematical theory of exclusive triplets. From (95) we find

$$(100) \qquad \begin{aligned} P(a_i.a_k.a_m) = P(a_i)\cdot P(a_i, a_k)\cdot P(a_i.a_k, a_m) = 0 \\ i \neq k \neq m \end{aligned}$$

The added inequality is to mean that any two of the subscripts must be unequal. Assuming, in correspondence with (97) and (98), that $P(a_i)$ and $P(a_i, a_k)$ do not vanish, we derive

$$(101) \qquad\qquad P(a_i.a_k, a_m) = 0 \qquad i \neq k \neq m$$

Using the rule of elimination [1], we have

$$(102) \qquad P(a_i, a_k) = P(a_i, a_m)\cdot P(a_i.a_m, a_k) + P(a_i, \overline{a_m})\cdot P(a_i.\overline{a_m}, a_k)$$

With the help of (101) we find

$$(103) \qquad P(a_i, a_k) = P(a_i, \overline{a_m})\cdot P(a_i.\overline{a_m}, a_k) \qquad i \neq k \neq m$$

Since probabilities are ≤ 1, omission of the last probability expression cannot make the right-hand side smaller. Using the rule of the complement [2], we thus arrive at the inequality

$$(104) \qquad P(a_i, a_k) + P(a_i, a_m) \leq 1 \qquad i \neq k \neq m$$

This is the characteristic condition for exclusive triplets. In combination with the conditions (97)–(98) of separability, it leads to important consequences concerning contraposition of the statement (93).

By contraposition we shall understand any change in the position of the three letters 'a_1', 'a_2', 'a_3', in (93), including an interchange of the letters 'a_1' and 'a_2'. The latter operation is usually not called a contraposition; but it is convenient for the following discussion

---

[1] ThP, p. 76.
[2] ThP, p. 60.

to include it under this name. We then have 6 contrapositive forms of the serial implication (93). They result when any two letters interchange their position, while the negation line always remains on top of the last term and thus does not participate in the positional changes. The 6 forms can be ordered in 3 groups. A group can be defined, for instance, by the identity of the third term. But we can also define the groups by the identity of the first term, or of the second, or middle, term.

Using relation (104) in combination with (99), we immediately derive the following theorem:

Theorem 23. Of the two contrapositive forms

$$(105) \qquad a_k \supset (a_i \supset \overline{a_m}) \qquad a_m \supset (a_i \supset \overline{a_k})$$

at most one can be separable.

This theorem follows because (104) requires that if $P(a_i, a_k) > \frac{1}{2}$, we must have $P(a_i, a_m) < \frac{1}{2}$, and vice versa. [1] We thus find that at most 3 contrapositive forms can be separable. Of course, it is possible that none of the 6 forms is separable, or that only one, or only two, are separable. The theory concerns only the maximum possible number of such forms, which is three.

Let us now write down the 6 forms in groups given by the identity of the middle term:

$$(106) \quad \begin{array}{lll} 1.\ a_1 \supset (a_2 \supset \overline{a_3}) & 3.\ a_2 \supset (a_3 \supset \overline{a_1}) & 5.\ a_3 \supset (a_1 \supset \overline{a_2}) \\ 2.\ a_3 \supset (a_2 \supset \overline{a_1}) & 4.\ a_1 \supset (a_3 \supset \overline{a_2}) & 6.\ a_2 \supset (a_1 \supset \overline{a_3}) \end{array}$$

According to theorem 23, only one form from each group can be

---

[1] We see that theorem 23 is even derivable if we replace (97) and (98) by the much weaker condition $P(a_2, a_1) > \frac{1}{2}$. This result can also be stated as follows. The conditional contrary to fact is applied in a situation in which we know that 'a_1' and 'a_3' are true, whereas 'a_2' is false. The question arises: if 'a_2' were true, which of the two other statements of the exclusive triplet would still be true? We can answer it by the rule: if there is a statement 'a_n' ($n \neq 2$) for which $P(a_2, a_n) > \frac{1}{2}$, this statement may be regarded as remaining true. This rule is unique because of relation (104), i.e., the condition can be satisfied by only one of the two statements 'a_1' and 'a_3'. However, in order to make the rule consistent with the existing statistical conditions we would have to add requirement (98), as was shown in the discussion of (90), whereas (97) would be dispensable.

separable. There exist, however, further restrictions, which do not diminish the number of separable forms, but their combination.

These restrictions result from a theorem of the calculus of probability which we formulated in (88) and which may be transcribed for our present notation as follows:

$$(107) \qquad \frac{P(a_i, a_k)}{P(a_k, a_i)} = \frac{P(a_k)}{P(a_i)}$$

We conclude from this theorem:

$$(108) \qquad \text{if } P(a_i, a_k) \gtrless P(a_k) \text{ then } P(a_k, a_i) \gtrless P(a_i)$$

We can now prove that among the 3 separable forms, two must have the same first term, and that consequently one proposition is excluded from being the first term. To prove this, assume that

$$(109) \qquad P(a_1) \sim 1 \qquad\qquad P(a_3) \sim 1$$

and that form 1 of the set (106) is separable. We know that then (2) is not separable. Since we now have $P(a_2, a_3) < \frac{1}{2}$ according to (104), we have, because $P(a_3) \sim 1$ was assumed,

$$(110) \qquad P(a_2, a_3) < P(a_3)$$

Using (108) we infer that

$$(111) \qquad P(a_3, a_2) < P(a_2)$$

This result excludes the form 3. Thus in the second group only the form 4 can be separable. We therefore have 2 separable forms, namely 1 and 4, which have the same first term, namely a_1.

Now we can add only one of the forms of the last group; thus either 'a_3' or 'a_2' is excluded as first term. We can even derive that 6 is excluded. For if 6 were separable, 5 would not be separable; since we assumed in (109) that $P(a_3) \sim 1$, this would mean that $P(a_1, a_3) < P(a_3)$, because otherwise 5 would satisfy the conditions (97)–(98) of separability. Using the inference which led from the exclusion of 2 to that of 3, we could now infer that 4 is excluded. But this contradicts our previous result according to which in the second group only 4 can be separable. Therefore 6 cannot be separable, if there are 3 separable forms; and 5 must be separable.

We can even conclude that $P(a_2) < \frac{1}{2}$. From the separability of 1 and (108) we infer that $P(a_1, a_2) \geqq P(a_2)$. From the separability of 4 and (108)–(109) we infer that $P(a_1, a_3) \geqq P(a_3)$. Applying (104) to the form 6 we then find $P(a_1, a_2) < \frac{1}{2}$, and thus $P(a_2) < \frac{1}{2}$. The assumption that all three probabilities $P(a_1)$, $P(a_2)$, $P(a_3)$, are close to 1 is incompatible with the assumption that there are 3 separable forms.

These derivations show: if 3 forms are separable, and if form 1 is among them, then conditions (109) determine the whole set of separable forms; namely, the forms 1, 4, 5. However, the set 1, 4, 6, can also be separable; only we must then have $P(a_1) \sim 1$, $P(a_2) \sim 1$, $P(a_3) < \frac{1}{2}$. In this case, the set 1, 3, 6 would also be separable. Which of the latter two sets is separable depends then on the values of the probabilities $P(a_i, a_k)$. However, the set 1, 3, 5, cannot be separable, because it has three different first terms.

Corresponding derivations can of course be given for other selections of the subscripts. The result that among the separable forms, two must have the same first term, is independent of the choice of the subscripts. The set is determined if two probabilities $P(a_i)$ and $P(a_k)$ are close to 1, and in addition, one form is given from the group in which 'a_i' and 'a_k' are first terms.

Furthermore, we can now show that two of the separable forms must have the same last term. If two forms have the same first term 'a_i', they belong to different groups of (106); and the third group then has 'a_i' as middle term. Thus 'a_i' cannot be the third term. A similar conclusion is easily drawn for the common third term. We formulate these results as follows:

Theorem 24. The following relations hold for a serial implication:

1. At most three contrapositive forms are separable.

2. Two of them have the same first term.

3. Two of them have the same last term.

4. The term which occurs twice as first term, does not occur as third term.

5. The term which occurs twice as third term, does not occur as first term.

These results concerning separability and contraposition, which apply both to admissible and to semi-admissible implications, may now be illustrated by examples. The example concerning the shell hitting the house is written in form 1 of (106): if a shell hits the house, then if there are persons in the house, they will be killed. In form 2 this reads: if the persons were not killed, then if they were in the house the shell did not hit the house. Now assume that the persons were not killed and were not in the house. We would then refuse to say: if the persons had been in the house, the shell would have hit the house. We would maintain, rather, that then the persons would have been killed. Forms 4 and 6 are also separable for this example. For instance, if the persons were in the house and no shell hit it, we would say, using 6: if the shell had hit the house, the persons would have been killed. Forms 3 and 5, however, are here not separable.

Another example of form 1 is given by the statement: if this salt is sodium bicarbonate, then if it is put into water it dissolves. This form is separable. In form 3 this reads: if this salt is put into water, then if it does not dissolve it is not sodium bicarbonate. This form is also separable. Suppose the salt was put into water and dissolved. Now we would say: if it had not dissolved it would not have been sodium bicarbonate. Likewise, form 6 is separable, whereas the forms 2, 4, 5 are not separable. For instance form 5 reads: if this salt does not dissolve, then if it is sodium bicarbonate it has not been put into water. This is not separable. Suppose we know that the salt does not dissolve and is not sodium bicarbonate. We then would not say: if it had been sodium bicarbonate it would not have been put into water. We would rather say that it would dissolve. This illustration shows again the retroactive function of a conditional contrary to fact. [1]

For the derivation of theorems 23 and 24 it has been assumed that the general situation G is the same for all separable forms. As far as theorem 23 is concerned, it is easily seen that this assumption is satisfied. With respect to the form on the left in (105), we apply

---

[1] Similar examples were studied and analyzed in a related way by Nelson Goodman, who emphasized the need for a condition comparable to the above separability condition; 'The problem of counterfactual conditionals', *Journ. of Philos.* 44, 1947, pp. 119–120.

the conditional contrary to fact if 'a_i' is true, whereas 'a_k' and '$\overline{a_m}$' are false. With respect to the form on the right in (105), the conditional contrary to fact is applied if 'a_m' is true, whereas 'a_k' and '$\overline{a_i}$' are false. But these are identical situations. Thus the conclusion that there are at most three separable forms is unquestionable. But even if situation G is the same within each group of (106), we might question whether it has to be the same for all three groups. In that case, we could not derive that the sets 1, 3, 5, and 2, 4, 6, are excluded. It seems to be an empirical fact, however, that in the usage of language the identity of the situation G is tacitly assumed for all groups. This is confirmed by many illustrations, which can be easily constructed and which show, like the given ones, that theorem 24 is satisfied.

Some further theorems may now be derived. From (98) we derive immediately:

Theorem 25. If '$a_2 \supset \overline{a_1}$' is nomological, or if '$a_1 \supset \overline{a_2}$' is nomological, the implication (93) is not separable.

The two conditions named in this theorem are of course equivalent.

Theorem 26. If (93) is separable, then neither one of the implications

(112) $$b \supset (a_2 \supset \overline{a_1})$$
(113) $$c \supset (a_2 \supset a_3)$$

is separable for any statement 'b' or 'c' which makes these implications true.

For (112) this follows because the separability of (93) leads to

(114) $$P(a_2, a_1) \sim 1$$

Applying (104) and interpreting 'a_i' as 'a_2', 'a_k' as 'a_1', and 'a_m' as 'b', leads to $P(a_2, b) < \frac{1}{2}$, which violates (99) for 'b' in the place of 'a_1'. Similarly, the theorem follows for (113) because (114) leads with (104) to

(115) $$P(a_2, a_3) < \tfrac{1}{2} \qquad\qquad P(a_2, \overline{a_3}) > \tfrac{1}{2}$$

Since in (113) the third term is positive, (104) assumes for (113) the form

(116) $$P(a_2, c) + P(a_2, \overline{a_3}) \leqq 1$$

In combination with (115) this leads to $P(a_2, c) < \frac{1}{2}$, and thus (113) is not separable. For these proofs, we have assumed that the general situation G holding for (112)–(113) is the same as the one holding for (93). This is permissible because the existence of this situation is presupposed with the assumption that (93) is separable.

Theorem 26 leads to the following theorem:

Theorem 27. Of the two implications

(117) $$a_1 \supset (a_2 \supset \overline{a_3})$$

(118) $$a_4 \supset (a_2 \supset a_3)$$

at most one is separable.

This theorem transfers theorem 21 to relative implications and we thus have:

Theorem 28. Two contrary relative implications are not both separable.

The following stronger theorem can be derived:

Theorem 29. If

(119) $$P(a_2, a_1) = P(a_2, a_4)$$

then neither one of the implications (117)–(118) is separable.

This follows because (117)–(118) lead to the relation

(120) $$a_1 \supset (a_2 \supset \overline{a_4})$$

We can therefore apply (104) to the two probabilities occurring in (119), each of which is therefore at most $= \frac{1}{2}$. Thus condition (99) is not satisfiable by either one of the implications (117)–(118). Note that this proof can still be given if (119) is only approximately true.

An illustration where (118) is separable, whereas (117) is not, can be given as follows. Let (118) be the statement 'if there is a current in the wires (a_4), then if the man touches the wires (a_2), he will be killed (a_3)'. Let 'a_1' be the statement 'the man is 6 feet high and on the ground, and the wires are 20 feet high'. Then both (117) and (118) are admissible; but only (118) is separable. If someone were to use '$a_2 \supset \overline{a_3}$' of (117) as a counterfactual conditional, we would argue, 'if the man touched the wires, he would not be on the ground'.

As a further illustration we may use an example mentioned by Quine [1], who raises the question whether it can be ruled out as impermissible within a coherent theory:

(121)   If Bizet and Verdi had been compatriots, Bizet would have been Italian.

(122)   If Bizet and Verdi had been compatriots, Verdi would have been French.

The present theory rules these implications out as follows. Statement (121) presupposes the major antecedent, 'Verdi is Italian' (a_1); and (122), the major antecedent 'Bizet is French' (a_4). We thus have here two relative admissible implications with different major antecedents. The paradoxical character arises because we know that Frenchmen are not Italians. When we include this addition into the meaning of 'a_1' and 'a_4', and put 'a_2' for 'Bizet and Verdi are compatriots', we can rewrite (121)–(122) in the form

$$(123) \quad a_1 \supset (a_2 \supset \overline{a_4}) \qquad\qquad (124) \quad a_4 \supset (a_2 \supset \overline{a_1})$$

These are two contrapositive forms of the same implication, and theorem 23 says that at most one of them can be separable. However, since we can regard here condition (119) as satisfied, we can apply theorem 29; and therefore none of the two statements (121)–(122) can be asserted separately.

Transition from relative to absolute implications offers, of course, another simple solution. When we add to (121)–(122) the omitted major antecedents and combine each with the minor antecedent conjunctively, using the form (92), each implication (121)–(122) is made admissible and reasonable. The total statement is then of third order, whereas the implicans '$a_1 . a_2$' or '$a_4 . a_2$', is false of first order. In contrast, when we also add the major antecedent of the other implication and use the implicans '$a_1 . a_2 . a_4$', this implicans is false of third order, and the implication is no longer admissible.

---

[1] W. Quine, *Methods of Logic*, New York 1950, p. 15.

Implications concerning irrelevance can also be separable. Using the illustration given for (69), we may say 'if the metal had been red, it would also have expanded', as soon as we know the truth of the major antecedent, 'the metal is heated'. The conditions of separability can here very well be satisfied.

If two serial implications are given, each of which is separable,

$$(125) \qquad\qquad a_1 \supset (a_2 \supset \overline{a_3})$$

$$(126) \qquad\qquad b_1 \supset (b_2 \supset \overline{b_3})$$

the question arises whether the conjunction of the two relative implications is separable. If 'a_2' and 'b_2' are false, we may say: if 'a_2' had been true, '$\overline{a_3}$' would have been true; and if 'b_2' had been true, '$\overline{b_3}$' would have been true. Can we now proceed to the conclusion: if 'a_2' and 'b_2' had been true, '$\overline{a_3}$' and '$\overline{b_3}$' would have been true? Obviously, the latter statement can only be asserted if '$a_2.b_2$' satisfies condition (98) with respect to '$a_1.b_1$', i.e., if

$$(127) \qquad\qquad P(a_2.b_2,\ a_1.b_1) \geqq P(a_1.b_1)$$

But this relation cannot be derived from the separability of the individual implications (125)–(126). We shall therefore say that, though the juxtaposition of the two relative implications is permissible if (125) and (126) are separable, their conjunction is separable only if, in addition, (127) is satisfied.

An example where the conjunction is not separable can be constructed as follows. Let (125) be the statement used previously, 'if this salt is sodium bicarbonate, then if it is put into water it will dissolve'; and let (126) be given by the statement 'if this salt is put into hot concentrated sulphuric acid and the solution is then cooled, then if it is barium sulphate, certain crystals will be deposited'. Each of these serial implications is separable. Now assume that the salt is sodium bicarbonate and that it is put into hot concentrated sulphuric acid and then cooled. Each implication is still separable; but we cannot proceed to saying: 'if the salt had been put into water and had been barium sulphate, then it would have dissolved and certain crystals would have been deposited'. This statement is false, because barium sulphate is not soluble in water. It is easily seen that (127) is not satisfied because '$b_2 \supset \bar{a}_1$' is nomological.

These considerations may be used for the discussion of relative equivalences, or double implications. Assume we have

(128) $$a_1 \supset (a_2 \equiv \bar{a}_3)$$

This can also be written in the four forms

(129a) $$a_1 \supset (a_2 \supset \bar{a}_3).(\bar{a}_3 \supset a_2)$$

(129b) $$a_1 \supset (a_2 \supset \bar{a}_3).(\bar{a}_2 \supset a_3)$$

(129c) $$a_1 \supset (a_3 \supset \bar{a}_2).(\bar{a}_3 \supset a_2)$$

(129d) $$a_1 \supset (a_3 \supset \bar{a}_2).(\bar{a}_2 \supset a_3)$$

If each of the two relative implications of (129a) is to be separable, the following relations must hold:

(130) $$P(a_1) \sim 1, \quad P(a_2, a_1) \geqq P(a_1), \quad P(\bar{a}_3, a_1) \geqq P(a_1)$$

These conditions are satisfiable. The conjunctive form

(131) $$a_2.\bar{a}_3 \supset \bar{a}_3.a_2$$

is here a tautology; thus condition (127) is certainly satisfied. Therefore the double implication of (129a), i.e., the conjunction of these relative implications, is separable if each of the implications is separable.

A similar result is derivable for (129d). However, in order that these implications be separable, we have to require that

(132) $$P(a_1) \sim 1, \quad P(\bar{a}_2, a_1) \geqq P(a_1), \quad P(a_3, a_1) \geqq P(a_1)$$

If both the conditions (130) and (132) are to be satisfied, we have to cancel the larger-than sign in all these relations. [1]

If each of the relative implications of (129b) is to be separable, we must have

(133) $$P(a_2, a_1) = P(\bar{a}_2, a_1) = P(a_1)$$

---

[1] See ThP, p. 79. The remarks following there the relation (11b) can be easily transcribed for the absolute notation.

because it is easily seen that the larger-than sign cannot hold in this case. The conjunctive form

(134) $a_2.\overline{a_2} \supset \overline{a_3}.a_3$

is here again tautological, and thus does not need the major antecedent 'a_1'. But since the implicans of (134) is false of third order, this implication is inadmissible. Similar conclusions can be drawn for (129c).

Since the two conjunctive forms of (129a) and (129d) are tautological and uninteresting, whereas the other two conjunctive forms are inadmissible, we shall renounce the use of conjunctions of implications for the relative equivalence of (128), and shall introduce the following definitions:

Definition 43.   A relative admissible equivalence is *separable*, if each of its implications is separable.

Definition 44.   An equivalence is *permissible* if it is admissible or if it is relative admissible and separable.

Definition 43 leads to the theorem:

Theorem 30.   The equivalence (128) is separable if the following conditions are satisfied

(135)
$$P(a_1) \sim 1, \; P(a_2, a_1) = P(\overline{a_2}, a_1) = P(a_1)$$
$$P(a_3, a_1) = P(\overline{a_3}, a_1) = P(a_1)$$

We see that the separability of an equivalence requires irrelevance, and thus excludes not only negative, but also positive relevance. Conditions (135) guarantee that each of the implications on the right in (129a–d) can be asserted separately. It can happen, of course, that only some, or none, of these forms are separable. In that case, we would not call the form (128) separable.

In practical applications of nomological statements, the theory of relative implications that are separable plays an important part, because it allows us to account for many cases of everyday usage of language in which we employ implications for conditionals contrary to fact although they do not directly represent laws of nature. Of this kind are statements like 'if Peter had known that Paul would come, he would not have come', or 'if John had set

his alarm clock in the evening, John would have awoken at 7 a.m.',
and many others. We can regard these statements as relative-
admissible implications that are separable, if we assume a major
antecedent that is comprehensive enough to make the serial
implication a law of nature, including psychological laws. For
instance, for the alarm-clock example we would have to assume
that the clock is correctly wired, that there is electric current in
the wire, that John's hearing is normal, that he is in good health,
etc. We do not have a perfect proof that these conditions are
satisfied; but their satisfaction appears highly probable in the
general situation G in which we use these implications. The theory
of separable relative implications thus allows us to employ nomological statements in situations in which we merely have a probable
knowledge that the conditions of their use are satisfied.

Some remarks concerning tautological implications may be
added. It is a trivial consequence of definition 40 that every
statement is admissible relative to itself, since '$a \supset a$' is an
admissible tautology [see (68)]. For instance, using the modality
of necessity for a characterization of nomological statements, we
may say: if it rains, it is necessary that it rains. The meaning of
the word 'necessary' used here, however, is not that of an absolute,
but of a relative modality. Thus we cannot conclude that the
raining is necessary in the sense that determinists would like to
say; raining is necessary only if it rains, and only relative to this
fact. A more familiar expression of this kind would be given by
the form: 'on a rainy day it rains, of course'; which means the same
as: 'on a rainy day it necessarily rains'. There is no objection to
admitting this usage.

These results cannot be used, however, to make an implication
separable relative to itself. Although the statement

(136) $$(a \supset b) \supset (a \supset b)$$

is an admissible tautology, the secondary implication is here not
separable. We have [1]

(137) $P(a \supset b) = 1 - P(a)[1 - P(a, b)]$
(138) $P(a, a \supset b) = P(a, \bar{a} \vee b) = P(a, b)$

---

[1] ThP, p. 88.

If $P(a) = 1$, the right-hand sides of (137) and (138) are identical; if $P(a) < 1$, the right-hand side of (137) is larger because the subtracted term is smaller. We therefore have

$$(139) \qquad\qquad P(a, a \supset b) \leqq P(a \supset b)$$

If the secondary implication is to be used as a conditional contrary to fact, 'a' must sometimes be false; therefore $P(a) < 1$. Then the equality sign in (139) is excluded, and (139) contradicts the separability condition (98).

Turning to other tautological implications, we find that the admissible implication

$$(140) \qquad\qquad a \supset (\bar{a} \supset c)$$

is not separable because $P(\bar{a}, a) = 0$ and thus condition (99) is violated. This result excludes the secondary implication of (140) from reasonable implications. Note that the form '$a.\bar{a} \supset c$', in which the two antecedents of (140) are conjoined, is not admissible, because it is not reduced. When (140) is accepted as admissible, this means merely that the major implication of (140) is regarded as reasonable. And this appears plausible as soon as the secondary implication is interpreted adjunctively; this is seen if the latter implication is replaced by '$a \lor c$' in an adjunctive meaning. The major implication of (140) is thus very different from that of '$a.\bar{a} \supset c$'.

When we substitute '$\bar{c}$' for the free variable 'c' in (140) and apply contraposition to the secondary implication, we arrive at the admissible tautology

$$(141) \qquad\qquad a \supset (c \supset a)$$

This implication is separable if $P(c, a) \geqq P(a) \sim 1$, according to (97)–(98). On this condition, in fact, there is no objection to using '$c \supset a$' counterfactually. Major antecedent and consequent are identical in (141); thus if 'a' is true and 'c' is false, the conditional contrary to fact '$c \supset a$' is merely of the noninterference kind. We saw in (87) that for a counterfactual of this kind the probability condition $P(c, a) \geqq P(a)$ is sufficient.

This discussion shows that the two so-called paradoxes of

adjunctive implication, formulated in (140) and (141), do not offer any difficulties to the theory of relative implications. It is the secondary implication, not the major one, which creates the paradox. But in (140) the secondary implication is not accepted as reasonable in this theory because this implication is not separable. In contrast, the secondary implication of (141) is accepted as reasonable if the separability condition is satisfied; and on that condition this implication appears reasonable because it then merely expresses an 'if' of noninterference.

Finally, we will consider the tautological admissible implication

$$(142) \qquad a.b \supset (a \supset b)$$

If 'a' and 'b' are true, it is separable because

$$(143) \qquad P(a.b) = P(a) \cdot P(a, b)$$

$$(144) \qquad P(a, a.b) = P(a, b)$$

and thus, $P(a)$ being ≤ 1,

$$(145) \qquad P(a, a.b) \geq P(a.b)$$

This relation satisfies the separability condition (98). Now (142) cannot be used counterfactually because it is separable only if 'a' is true. However, it is applied in other ways.

To give an illustration, we shall use a slightly more complicated example which requires the use of the functional notation. Suppose it is known that a man x who committed a certain crime [statement '$f(x)$'] has an old scar on his left leg [statement '$g(x)$']. A man is arrested [statement '$a(y)$'] under the suspicion of being this criminal. Now consider the implication:

(146)   If the arrested man has committed the crime, he has a scar on his left leg.

In order to symbolize it, let us use a superscript to indicate that the extension of a function is at most $= 1$; for 'f' we use the abbreviation

$$(147a) \qquad f^{(1)}(x) =_{Df} f(x).(z)[f(z) \supset (z = x)]$$

which applies similarly to the function 'a'. We can now write the following tautological implication, which contains the free variables 'x' and 'y':

(147b) $f^{(1)}(x).g(x).a^{(1)}(y) \supset [f(y) \supset g(y)]$

We have here omitted the existential assertion expressed in the phrases 'the criminal' and 'the arrested man'. Now assume we know that there is an x and there is an y such that the major implicans is true. Let us investigate whether the secondary implication '$f(y) \supset g(y)$', which corresponds to (146), is then separable.

Assume first that the arrested man is, in fact, the criminal, i.e., assume $y = x$. Then the separability condition (98) is satisfied. This follows by the use of inferences analogous to relations (143)–(145), since it is easily seen that the addition of a statement on the left in (142) has no influence upon the resulting inequality. The relative implication '$f(x) \supset g(x)$' is therefore separable. However, separability no longer obtains for the contrapositive form:

(148)   if the arrested man has no scar on his left leg, he has not committed the crime,

which is part of the total implication

(149) $f(x).g(x).a^{(1)}(y) \supset [\overline{g(y)} \supset \overline{f(y)}]$

When we put here $y = x$, the minor antecedent '$\overline{g(x)}$' contradicts the major antecedent, and condition (98) is violated. The relative implication '$\overline{g(x)} \supset \overline{f(x)}$' is therefore not separable. This result corresponds to usage, since we would not be willing to accept (148) in the counterfactual meaning: 'if the man did not have a scar on his left leg, he would not have committed the crime'.

Assume, secondly, that $y \neq x$ and that the arrested man neither is the criminal nor has a scar. In this case, the form (147b) is not separable, since the minor antecedent '$f(y)$' contradicts the major antecedent in case $y \neq x$. In fact, we would not say, 'if this man y had committed the crime, he would have a scar on his left leg', since the scar has no causal relation to the crime; instead, we would rather conclude that the major antecedent is false. In contrast, the form (149) is here separable, since the minor antecedent '$\overline{g(y)}$' does not contradict the major one for $y \neq x$, but is irrelevant to it. And the form (148) thus appears reasonable.

We see that we cannot lay down separability conditions for the indefinite forms (147b) and (149); which one of the two is separable depends upon the identification of y. It appears that, as long as this identification is unknown, common usage would accept both forms (146) and (148). Such usage can perhaps be explained as an *alternating meaning*. The clause 'if the arrested man has committed the crime' in (146) is meant to include the tacit addition, 'and if $y = x$'; in contrast, the clause 'if the arrested man has no scar' in (148) is meant to include the tacit addition, 'and if $y \neq x$'. But as soon as the identification is known, we proceed to either using (146) or (148). We see that a counterfactual use of these implications, i.e., a use contrary to known identification, is excluded for the formulations given.

It is different when we put an identity statement in the place of '$f(y)$' and replace the two statements (146) and (148) by the following ones:

(150a)   if the arrested man is identical with the criminal, he has a scar on his left leg.

(150b)   if the arrested man does not have a scar on his left leg, he is not identical with the criminal.

With reference to (147b) we can write the corresponding total implications, when we omit again the existential assertion of the definite descriptions,

(151a) $f^{(1)}(x) . g(x) . a^{(1)}(y) \supset [(x = y) \supset g(y)]$

(151b) $f^{(1)}(x) . g(x) . a^{(1)}(y) \supset [\overline{g(y)} \supset (x \neq y)]$

These formulations, in which the identity assumption is explicitly stated or denied, respectively, are both separable, and both have the same meaning. For this reason, the two forms (150a–b) can also be used counterfactually; for instance, we can say: 'if the arrested man had not had a scar on his left leg, he would not have been identical with the criminal'.

These considerations show that a merely adjunctive implication, such as (150a) or (150b), can be made reasonable by being used as a relative implication within a serial implication, even if the latter is a tautology. It is reasonable relative to the facts known; and the relation to the facts is here analytic.

IX

PERMISSIBLE AND PROPER IMPLICATION

In order to indicate the object language equivalent of a nomological operation, I used in ESL, p. 377, a grave accent. This notation may be taken over for the present theory. In application to implication, it leads to the following definition, which applies likewise to all other operations:

Definition 45. The statement '$a \overset{\backprime}{\supset} b$' is true if and only if '$a \supset b$' is a nomological statement. (I-term.)

It appears desirable to introduce a similar notation for the class of admissible statements. We shall use here an acute accent and, examplifying it for the 'or', introduce the following definition, which applies likewise to the exclusive 'or' and the 'and':

Definition 46. The statement '$a \overset{\backprime}{\vee} b$' is true if and only if '$a \vee b$' is an admissible statement. (V-term.)

For implications and equivalences, we apply an analogous notation to the wider class of permissible operations of this kind, which in addition to admissible statements includes certain statements of first order and which was defined in definitions 42 and 44. This leads to the following definition, which applies likewise to equivalences:

Definition 47. The statement '$a \overset{\prime}{\supset} b$' is true if and only if '$a \supset b$' is a permissible implication. (V-term.)

Definitions 45–47 are not definitions in the usual sense, because they connect two levels of language. They may be called shifted definitions, since they involve what Carnap has called a shift of the level of language.

In definition 47, the statement containing an accent implication is introduced as a truth-functional parallel of the metalinguistic statement to which it corresponds. If the metalinguistic statement is true or false, then the accent implication is true, or false, although of course in the second case the adjunctive implication still may be true. We speak here of an *equipollence of meanings*.

There exists a second way of introducing a reasonable implication, according to which an 'if–then' statement has a *restricted
meaning*. It is meaningful only if certain metalinguistic conditions
for the corresponding adjunctive implication are satisfied, but
otherwise it is meaningless. This conception of meaning requires
some comment. When we regard an expression like '$f(f)$' as meaningless, we can find this out from the formation rules of our language.
It is different with the implications considered here: whether they
are meaningful, or meaningless, depends on empirical conditions.
As far as admissible implications are concerned, these conditions
are collected in the system S_0 of laws of nature, which laws determine, not only whether '$a \supset b$' is nomological, but also whether it
is admissible, because they determine the status of the disjunctive
residuals of '$a \supset b$'. As far as relative admissible implications are
concerned, the empirical conditions referred to even include mat-
ters of fact, expressed in the high probability of the major antecedent, and in addition, the conditions of separability. We therefore
can assign meaning to such an implication only when the empirical
conditions are known to be satisfied. I will speak here of *physical
meaning*. [1]

An implication of this kind will be called *proper implication*.
Since it will be denoted by an arrow, it may also be called *arrow-
implication*. A sentence '$a \rightarrow b$' is an ambivalent expression; it
may be true, false, or meaningless, depending on certain empirical
conditions. The definition of proper implication is given as follows

Definition 48.

α)   The statement '$a \rightarrow b$' is true if and only if '$a \supset b$' is permissible.

β)   The statement '$a \rightarrow b$' is false if and only if '$a \rightarrow \bar{b}$' is true.

γ)   In all other cases, '$a \rightarrow b$' is meaningless.

The arrow implication, or proper implication, is especially suited
for the expression of a conditional contrary to fact. To illustrate
the difference between accent-implication and arrow-implication,
we may refer to the examples given in the discussion of theorems

---

[1] This term was introduced in my book *Experience and Prediction*,
Chicago 1938, p. 40.

20–21. The statement 'if an ice cube of 86° is heated, it contracts' is false when regarded as representing an accent implication, because it is not admissible; and the statement 'if an ice cube of 86° is heated, it does not contract' is then also false. If regarded as representing arrow, or proper, implication, however, both these sentences are meaningless. The latter conception appears preferable to the former because the statements convey contradictory information about what would happen to the hypothetical ice cube, and therefore do not convey any information but that ice cubes of 86° cannot exist. If it is irrelevant what we put into the implicate, however, it appears reasonable to regard the implication as having no meaning. This is also illustrated by the examples (121)–(122).

The question may be raised whether we can regard the category *meaningless*, or *physically meaningless*, as a third truth-value, comparable to the truth value *indeterminate* of quantum mechanics. For this part of physics, such an interpretation appears advisable for the following reasons. Quantum-mechanical statements which are indeterminate cannot be judged to be so before it is known whether certain observations have, or have not, been made. Such statements must therefore be retained in the language of the scientist until the time arises that their logical status can be ascertained, and thus should pertinently be regarded as meaningful and merely capable of assuming a specific truth value of indeterminacy.

For proper implications, a corresponding situation does not exist as far as they are given by admissible implications. In using these implications, we need not wait for further observations, once they have been generally established. Their logical status is ascertainable on the basis of the system S_0 and thus can be found out before specific observations concerning the event referred to have been made.

A different situation arises only for relative admissible implications, in particular, because we have to know that the major antecedent is highly probable before we can use them. However, a way out of this difficulty is found as follows: as long as the probability of the major antecedent or the satisfaction of the condition of separability is unknown, we use the form (92), i.e., '$a.b \supset c$', and thus replace the relative implication by an absolute admissible implication. This corresponds to usage of language. For instance, if it is unknown whether a certain salt is sodium bicarbonate, we would not say: 'if it is put into water it will dissolve'. We would say: 'if this is sodium bicarbonate and it is put into water it will dissolve'. We thus can always avoid the use of relative implications as long as the conditions of their meaningfulness have not yet been ascertained. For these reasons, I would not advocate the introduction of a three-valued logic for proper implications, although, of course, it could very well be done.

Let us now consider an illustration where we deny the existence of a reasonable implication. We select an example where an absolute implication is concerned. Assume someone says, 'if Peter starts his new job on a Friday, he will soon be dismissed'. If we regard this statement as a proper implication, we can tell that it is meaningless before we know whether Peter does start his job on a Friday, and whether or not he is soon fired. The man who uttered the prophetic sentence believes that it expresses a law of nature, and thus the sentence has *logical meaning* for him, because it is no contradiction to assume that such a natural law exists. He uses a system S different from S_0. When we refuse to accept his statement as meaningful, we do so because we have good evidence that S_0 does not contain such a law, and thus classify his sentence as *physically meaningless*.

Using the accent implication, we would classify the sentence as false. If the implicans is true, i.e., if the implication is not used contrary to fact, it may appear as a matter of taste which of the two implications should be used for the interpretation. However, it is a disadvantage of the interpretation by the accent implication that, if the implication is false, we cannot infer that the contrary implication is true. For the arrow implication this inference can be made.

There exists a third interpretation of the sentence, which I have called *semi-adjunctive* implication. [1] In this interpretation, the implication is verified or falsified as an adjunctive implication if the implicans is true. Only if the implicans is not true is it classified

---

[1] ESL, § 64.

either as an accent or an arrow implication. This mixed procedure offers perhaps the best correspondence to actual usage in the case considered. The example shows that usage can be so vague as to make a unique interpretation impossible.

For operations involving the arrow implication, the following rules can be collected. If the arrow implications are all of the absolute kind, theorem 14 allows us to divide a conjunction of arrow implications into individual implications; theorem 15, vice versa, allows for a composition of individual arrow implications of the same order into a conjunction; theorem 16 makes possible certain other forms of division and composition of implications; theorem 19 allows for transitivity if the implications have the same order. In the composition process, however, we always have to face the possibility that reducing may be required. For relative implications, analogous theorems hold only if certain conditions of separability are satisfied that go beyond the separability of the individual implications.

Furthermore, it was shown that contraposition is subject to serious limitations; we refer to theorem 17–18 and 23–24. And in the discussion of (80) and (81) it was shown that the invariance principle of implication does not hold for admissible implications.

This survey shows that the operations with proper implications are rather limited and require attention to the distinction between various kinds and orders, and to possible reducing. It is therefore not possible to construct a practicable calculus of arrow-implication. In general, if we want to construct derivations, we have to use the familiar adjunctive calculus; and we then must check for individual results whether they can be interpreted by arrow-implications. The class of statements which conversational language regards as reasonable is not complete; in order to construct derivative relations between statements of this class we have to go beyond the class.

This is the reason that logicians are inclined to regard the definition of reasonable operations as unnecessary. I cannot share this view. The formal definition of statements that have the appeal of intuitive meanings is a problem worthy of the study of the logician, even though our language cannot be restricted to such statements. Without a theory of admissible operations, neither the analysis of every-day language nor that of scientific language would be complete; and many questions concerning the meaning of common-sense terms and scientific terms could not be answered. Moreover, the explication of the term 'law of nature', which goes beyond that of the term 'reasonable operation', is indispensable for the analysis of science.

Since the present monograph is written with the intention to give an explication of these terms, it remains to justify the proposed explicans, i.e., to show that if this explicans is assumed, the usage of language is compatible with human behavior. For permissible implications, this amounts to showing that the use of conditionals contrary to fact is justifiable if these conditionals satisfy the requirements for these implications. Such a proof is important because conditionals contrary to fact have widespread practical applications. For instance, when after an automobile accident the driver of a car is sentenced to jail because he did not use his brakes, this sentence is based on the conditional contrary to fact, 'if the man had stepped on the brake, the car would have stopped'. Our theory classifies this implication as permissible. However, why are we justified to put a man into jail because a certain implication is not only true, but satisfies certain formal requirements?

I think this question can be answered as follows. A conditional contrary to fact is justifiable if, in case the implicans were true, the implication would still hold. Now this condition of adequacy, reasonable as it may appear, offers a serious difficulty: it can be used only if it is meant as a reasonable implication. Thus it presupposes an explication of such implications in order to be applicable. In fact, if the given condition of adequacy is interpreted as an adjunctive interpretation, it is obviously true when the original implication is merely adjunctive.

The condition of adequacy, therefore, must be stated in a different form. This can be done as follows. In order to make a synthetic implication '$a \supset b$' applicable for a conditional contrary to fact, we shall require that, if 'a' is true, the implication '$a \supset b$' is not made false by a law of nature; in other words, that the implication

(152) $$a \supset \overline{a \supset b}$$

must not be a law of nature. In this formulation, our condition of adequacy does not presuppose the concept of permissible implication, but only that of nomological implication, or law of nature. It is easily seen that our explication satisfies this condition. The formula (152) is tautologically equivalent to the form $a \supset \bar{b}$'; thus our condition of adequacy amounts to requiring that the contrary implication must not be a nomological statement. It was shown that permissible implications satisfy this condition.

This justification presupposes an explication of the term 'law of nature'. If this appears undesirable, we may formulate the condition of adequacy by saying that there should be no inductive evidence for the implication (152) apart from the inductive evidence used for the establishment of '$\bar{a}$'. Since our nomological statements are defined in a way satisfying this condition, we can refer to this widest form of a condition of adequacy for the justification of our explication of reasonable implications.

This remark opens the path for a justification of our explication of 'law of nature'. The use of this term appears justifiable if laws of nature are constructed from observations by inductive methods, and thus can be used for the purpose of prediction. This condition is satisfied by our explication (see ESL pp. 359–360). The justification of the explicans 'nomological statement' is thus reduced to the general problem of the justification of inductive methods, a solution of which I have given in other publications.

These considerations show that the given explication of the terms 'law of nature' and 'reasonable operation' is justifiable. With this remark I do not wish to say that the proposed explication is the only one satisfying conditions of adequacy, or that all individual features of this explication are covered by this justification. However, I do believe that, on the whole, our usage of language can be accounted for in terms of this explication. In extending and improving my previous investigations, the present paper is an attempt to reach this very aim — carried through in full knowledge of the limitations imposed upon any such undertaking.

APPENDIX

GENUINE PROBABILITIES AND THE INDUCTIVE VERIFICATION OF
ALL-STATEMENTS

A probability expression is written in the form

(153) $$P(A, B) = p$$

where A is the *reference class* and B the *attribute class*. For instance, A may be the class of persons who are 21 years old, B the class of persons dying within this year. Probability is always interpreted as the limit of a relative frequency within a sequence; thus we have

(154) $$P(A, B) = \lim_{n \to \infty} \frac{N^n(A \cdot B)}{N^n(A)}$$

where the symbol 'N^n' means: 'number up to the n-th element of the sequence'. For all practical uses, it is sufficient to replace the concept of limit by that of a practical limit; I refer to another publication [1].

The value p of the limit cannot be ascertained by counting the whole sequence, because the sequence is either infinitely long, or too long to be actually counted; in fact, if a probability is to be used for predictions, we have to know the limit long before the sequence is finished. The following two ways offer themselves.

First, the value of the limit is found by counting an initial section of the sequence and extending the observed relative frequency to future observations in terms of an inductive inference. We speak here of a direct method, or a *direct probability*. For the use of this method we introduce the following definitions.

Definition I. A member x of a sequence has been *examined* with regard to the attribute B, if individual observations have been made which allow us to state directly, or to infer deductively, whether x belongs to B.

---

[1] ThP, p. 347.

For instance, if it is known that x belongs to B, we also know that x does not belong to $\overline{B}$.

Definition II. A reference class is *open* with respect to the attribute B if the number of its members is large as compared with the number of members which have been examined individually with respect to B.

Definition III. A reference class is *statistically known* with respect to the attribute B if a sufficient number of its elements has been examined with respect to B so as to enable us to make an inductive inference concerning the distribution in the total class.

Definition IV. A probability is *direct* if it has been ascertained by an inductive inference in a reference class which is open and statistically known.

The condition that the reference class must be statistically known (definition III) is a rather strong condition. The requirement that a sufficient number of elements be examined refers to the use of standard inductive procedures in terms of which we decide when the number of observations is large enough to admit of an inductive inference; among such procedures, cross induction plays an important part. (See ThP, § 86 and p. 430). These considerations make it obvious that the verification of nomological statements belongs in what I have called *advanced knowledge* (ThP, p. 364).

We now turn to the second, or indirect, method. It is used when the reference class, though open, is not statistically known; and it is also used when the reference class is empty. For the latter case, the value of (154) is indeterminate, and we can therefore assign any value to the probability [1]; but we shall introduce a method which leads here to a unique value, thus distinguishing one of the values from all the others as most appropriate. It should be noted that we do not consider other reference classes than either open or empty ones; i.e., we do not consider a reference class of a small but not vanishing number of elements, because they are unsuitable for predictions.

Definition V. A probability is *indirect* if it is ascertained,

---

[1] ThP, p. 56.

for an open or empty reference class, by deductive derivation from direct probabilities, or from admissible statements, or both.

Definition VI. A probability is *genuine* if it is direct or indirect.

Definition V may be illustrated by examples. Using an admissible statement, such as

(155) $(x)[x \in A \supset x \in B]$

We conclude that [1]

(156) $P(A, B) = 1$

This method can be used even if A is empty. Since the contrary implication of (155) then is not admissible, we arrive at a unique value for a probability within an empty reference class. Note that it would not suffice to require that (155) be tautological, because two contrary implications can be both tautological, and we then could likewise derive that $P(A, B) = 0$.

Suppose a physicist is making quantum-mechanical measurements of a certain kind (A) and computes that the probability of observing a certain value of a quantity B is $= p$. His computation may refer to a kind of measurement which has not yet been made; thus his reference class, though open and not empty because measurements will now be made, is statistically unknown. For his computation, he uses a law of nature which states that under such and such conditions the probability is $= p$. This law is formulated in an admissible statement; therefore definition V is satisfied. The physicist will even maintain that, if such measurements were made on the moon, they would lead to the same results. Since such measurements will presumably never be made, this reference class is empty; but an indirect probability is computed for it in a unique way.

The latter kind of inference can also be represented as follows.

---

[1] ThP, p. 54. This means that axiom II, 1 of my theory of probability is to be qualified, for genuine probabilities, by the condition that the implication '$(A \supset B)$' of this axiom must be admissible. Since the rule of the complement is then not derivable, this rule must be used as an additional axiom.

We may know a law of nature saying that for all classes C belonging in a class γ the following relation holds:

(157) $$P(A.C, B) = P(A, B)$$

Now the common class $A.C$ may be empty although A is not empty; yet a unique probability is assigned to it. Derivations within the calculus of probability also supply indirect probabilities. With the use of admissible statements, however, it is possible to derive probabilities inductively from direct probabilities. The calculus of probability offers no such methods; for instance, it does not give any rules how to go from $P(A, B)$ to $P(A.C, B)$. A statement like (157) is not derivable in the calculus; it represents an empirical assumption to be added to the premisses of the derivation. But it is not always possible to verify such an assumption directly by compiling statistics. By the use of admissible statements we are able to extend inductively the set of premisses which enter into the deductive derivations of the calculus of probability. It is of particular interest that in this way probabilistic methods are supplemented by schematized statement forms in which high probabilities have been replaced by admissible statements. The methods of deductive logic thus come to the help of probabilistic inferences and allow us to state conditions under which synthetic additions to compiled statistics are permissible.

The process of going from high probabilities to all-statements is never deductive; furthermore, the introduction of all-statements requires the satisfaction of more conditions than merely the existence of high probability value. This process must therefore be regarded as a *schematization*. We will now give a brief summary of the conditions on which this schematization is dependent. The all-statement to be introduced will be assumed to be written in the form (155).

The first condition of schematization is that

(158) $$P(A, B) \sim 1$$

and that this probability be genuine (definition VI). The latter requirement can be satisfied by beginning with direct probabilities. Once a number of original nomological statements has been constructed, these statements can be used for the computation of indirect probabilities, which in turn are employed for the construction of further original nomological statements of the synthetic kind. There is no circularity in such a procedure; on the contrary, the requirements laid down for original nomological statements supply a parallel to the requirement of genuine probabilities. The condition of exhaustiveness excludes empty reference classes. Furthermore, the condition of universality, and of unrestricted exhaustiveness, excludes small reference classes within which we can verify an all-statement through enumeration, thus making an inductive inference unnecessary; it assumes a function similar to the condition of an open reference class.

The second condition of schematization is that, in addition to (158), the relation

$$(159) \qquad P(\overline{B}, \overline{A}) \sim 1$$

be satisfied. This condition insures that the form (155) allows for contraposition. Relation (159) cannot be derived from (158) unless further conditions are specified. When we put

$$(160) \qquad P(A, B) = 1 - d, \qquad P(\overline{B}, \overline{A}) = 1 - d'$$

and use relation (88), we find

$$(161) \qquad \frac{P(A, \overline{B})}{P(\overline{B}, A)} = \frac{d}{d'} = \frac{1 - P(B)}{P(A)}$$

Therefore $d' \leqq d$ if and only if $P(A) \leqq 1 - P(B)$, or

$$(162) \qquad P(A) + P(B) \leqq 1$$

Relation (162) formulates the condition on which we can go from (158) to (159) while remaining within the same small deviation d from the value 1. The proof of (159) can therefore be given by proving (158) and (162). If $d = 0$, i.e., $P(A, B) = 1$, we see from (161) that $d' > 0$ requires $P(B) = 1$; therefore a proof that $d' = 0$ can here be given by showing that $P(B) < 1$. For this case, relation (162) is no longer derivable, and the value $P(A)$ is subject to no specific restrictions. But this case has no practical significance because we can never prove inductively that d is strictly $= 0$.

It should be noted that, although (162) allows us to go from (158) to (159), relation (162) is not sufficient to provide for a transition from (159) to (158). For the latter transition, it must be required that $d \leq d'$, and (161) shows that his leads to the condition $1 - P(B) \leq P(A)$, or

(163) $$P(A) + P(B) \geq 1$$

Conditions (162) and (163) are compatible only for the special case of the equality sign. In general, therefore, we can proceed only in one direction. For instance, if we know that (162) holds, a proof of (158) is a proof of (159), but not vice versa. In the usual application of inductive verification, the terms 'A' and 'B' are so defined that (162) is satisfied. This explains why confirming evidence for (158) is also confirming evidence for (159), whereas confirming evidence for (159) is not confirming evidence for (158). These considerations supply the answer to a so-called paradox of confirmation pointed out by C. Hempel. [1]

For instance, although the probability is not high that a house is red, it is highly probable that something not red is not a house. Here d' is very small, whereas d is not small, and making d' even smaller by further confirming evidence has scarcely any influence upon d. The ratio between d and d' is given by (161) and is rather large, because the number of things that are not red, i.e., $1 - P(B)$, is much larger than the number of houses, i.e., $P(A)$. Condition (162) is here satisfied. In this example, of course, nobody would assert that all houses are red, because too many instances to the contrary are known. However, consider the statement, 'all buildings made by man are lower than 1300 feet'. Although this statement is true up to the present time, we would not be willing to assert it for all times; the general probability that a building made by man be lower than 1300 feet can scarcely be estimated as high as 1. Its contrapositive, in contrast, expresses a high probability, since it is highly probable for all times that something not lower than 1300 feet will not be a building made by man. A confirming instance for this contrapositive form, for instance, a mountain that is higher than

---

[1] See ThP, p. 435.

1300 feet, will not change our estimate of the original form.

The third condition of schematization is that no exceptions to (155) be known and that we have no evidence that a class C can be defined by us such that

(164) $$P(A.C, B) < P(A, B)$$

This condition states that we should be unable to say on what conditions exceptions to the general implication (155) would occur. It would be too strong a condition to require that *there be* no exceptions. In some sense, there exists general evidence that exceptions will occur, because too many laws of physics have later turned out to be merely approximately true. But we must be unable to describe conditions upon which an exception to (155) could be expected. In other words, there should be no *specific evidence* that the general implication considered is subject to exceptions. If this condition is satisfied, the assumption that (155) is strictly true is at least compatible with available knowledge.

Calling a class C satisfying (164) an exception to the relation (158), we can derive the following relations for exceptions. Using a fundamental inequality of the calculus of probability [1]

(165) $$1 - \frac{1-P(A,B)}{P(A,C)} \leq P(A.C, B)$$

we find, solving this relation for $P(A, C)$ and applying the value d of (160):

(166) $$P(A, C) \leq \frac{d}{1-P(A.C,B)}$$

The denominator is here always > 0 because of (163). Therefore, $d = 0$ requires $P(A, C) = 0$, or in other words: if $P(A, B) = 1$, exceptions C can occur only in a zero-frequency. This means that even in this case exceptions are not impossible, but the limit of their relative frequency must be $= 0$. [2] If $d > 0$, exceptions can occur in a higher frequency $P(A, C)$, which, however, is subject to the restriction (166). In order to study this relation let us put

(167) $$P(A, C) = f, \qquad P(A, B) - P(A.C, B) = e$$

---

[1] ThP, p. 79, left part of equation (15). For the above form we have interchanged 'B' and 'C'.

[2] The class C can then still be infinite; see ThP, p. 72.

We call f the *frequency of the exception* C, and e the *degree of the exception* C. The denominator in (166) can then be written in the form $e + d$; solving (166) for d, we thus find

(168) $$\frac{f}{1-f} \cdot e \leqq d$$

This relation may be called the *restriction for exceptions*. It states that, for a small value d, a high degree e of exception is restricted to a low frequency f, and a high frequency f of exceptions is restricted to a low degree e. The highest degree of exception is assumed for $P(A.C, B) = 0$, for which case (166) furnishes $f \leqq d$; lower degrees of exception allow for a somewhat higher f, which however is controlled by (168).

These considerations show that a high probability $P(A, B)$ is no guarantee for the absence of exceptions. If we can prove that $P(A, B)$ is close to 1 within the interval d, we know that exceptions are subject to restriction (168); but they may exist. Even if we could show that $d = 0$, exceptions could still occur, though they are limited to a zero-frequency. It follows that a proof for the absence of exceptions must be based on considerations involving other evidence than merely evidence for a high value of $P(A, B)$.

It is in this connection that the requirement of universality, laid down for original nomological statements, assumes a most important function. If an all-statement is restricted to a certain space-time region, there may exist special conditions in this region which make the all-statement true, whereas it may be false for other regions. If we can maintain, without any restriction to individuals or individual space-time regions, that condition (158) is true, it appears improbable that we could ever define a class C for which (164) holds. Thus universality represents some guarantee that, as is required for all-statements, not even a zero-frequency class of exceptions exists.

The rules laid down in the definition of admissible implications serve therefore as an instrument to equip such implications with inductive validity and the prospect of truth without exceptions. It is for this reason that such implications can be used for predictions and for conditionals contrary to fact.

BIBLIOGRAPHY

BAYLIS, C., 'The Given and Perceptual Knowledge', *Philosophic Thought in France and the United States*, Buffalo: University of Buffalo Publications in Philosophy, 1950, pp. 181–201.

BEARDSLEY, E. L., '"Non-accidental" and counter-factual sentences', *Journal of Philosophy*, 46 (1949), pp. 573–591.

BURKS, A., 'The Logic of Causal Propositions', *Mind*, 60 (1951), pp. 363–382.

CARNAP, R., 'Testability and Meaning', *Philosophy of Science*, 3 (1936), pp. 419–471; 4 (1937), pp. 2–40.

————, *The Logical Syntax of Language*, New York: Harcourt, Brace and Co., 1937, § 69.

————, *Meaning and Necessity*, University of Chicago Press, 1947.

CHISHOLM, R., 'The Contrary-to-fact Conditional', *Mind*, 55 (1946), pp. 289–307.

DIGGS, B. J., 'Counterfactual Conditionals', *Mind*, 61 (1952), pp. 513–527.

GOODMAN, N., 'A Query on Confirmation', *Journal of Philosophy*, 43 (1946), pp. 383–385.

————, 'The Problem of Counterfactual Conditionals', *Journal of Philosophy*, 44 (1947), pp. 113–128.

HAMPSHIRE, S., 'Subjunctive Conditionals', *Analysis*, 9 (1948), pp. 9–14.

HEMPEL, C. and OPPENHEIM, P., 'Studies in the Logic of Explanation', *Philosophy of Science*, 15 (1948), pp. 135–175.

LEWIS, C. I., *Analysis of Knowledge and Valuation*, La Salle, Illinois, Open Court Publishing Co., 1947, pp. 219–253.

———— and LANGFORD, C. H., *Symbolic Logic*, New York and London: The Century Co., 1932, Ch. VII.

PEIRCE, C. S., *Collected Papers*, v. II (Elements of Logic), Cambridge, Mass.: Harvard University Press, 1932, p. 199.

POPPER, K. R., 'A Note on Natural Laws and so-called "contrary-to-fact Conditionals"', *Mind*, 58 (1949), pp. 62–66.

RAMSEY, F. P., *Foundations of Mathematics*, New York: Harcourt, Brace and Co., 1931, pp. 237–257.

REICHENBACH, H., *Elements of Symbolic Logic*, New York: MacMillan Co., 1947, Ch. VIII, quoted as ESL.

————, *Theory of Probability*, Berkeley and Los Angeles: University of California Press, 1949, quoted as ThP.

RUSSEL, B. and WHITEHEAD, A. N., *Principia Mathematica*, I, Cambridge University Press, 1925, pp. 20–22.

————, *The Principles of Mathematics*, New York: W. W. Norton and Co., 1938, pp. 492–493.

SIMON, H. A., 'On the Definition of the Causal Relation', *Journal of Philosophy*, 49, 1952, pp. 517–528.

WEINBERG, JULIUS, 'Contrary-to-fact Conditionals', *Journal of Philosophy*, 48 (1951), pp. 17–22.

WILL, F. L., 'The Contrary-to-fact Conditional', *Mind*, 56 (1947), pp. 236–249.

TABLE OF THEOREMS

TABLE OF DEFINITIONS

TABLE OF DEFINITIONS IN THE APPENDIX

INDEX

admissible: 75;
  fully, 71, 75, 79;
  relative to p, 95;
  semi-, 71, 73, 74, 75, 78, 79
all-statement:
  proper, 40
analytic, 19
antecedent:
  major, 96, 98;
  minor, 96, 98

binary-connected, 20, 21

calculus:
  of functions, 5;
  lower functional, 11, 18;
  completeness of, 11;
  of propositions, 25, 60
Carnap, R., 5
causal relation, 4
C-form: 27, 28, 41, 61;
  elongated, 29
class:
  attribute, 126;
  reference, 126;
  open, 127
closed, 19
conditional contrary to fact: 7, 8,
  14, 19, 68, 83, 86, 112, 120, 124;
  primary, 96;
  reasonable, 90;
  regular, 88;
  secondary, 96
confirmation:
  paradox of, 131
conjunctive:
  non-, 71
consequent, 96
contractible, 20, 21
contraction, 20, 23

contradiction, 29
contraposition, 77, 78, 102, 106, 123
counterfactuals: 92
  of non-interference, 88, 90, 99,
  101

datum:
  observational, 85
description, definite, 35, 36
D-form: 27, 28, 41, 43, 44, 45, 46,
  47, 48, 68;
  elongated, 29

entailment:
  logical, 1;
  physical, 1, 5
equipollence: 11;
  of meanings, 119
equipollent, 10, 16, 19
equisignificance, 21
equisignificant, 19, 20
equivalence:
  relative, 112;
  relative admissible, 112
exhaustive:
  in elementary terms, 30, 50;
  in major terms, 30, 49;
  non-, 45;
  quasi-, 67, 69, 70, 72, 73;
  unrestrictedly, 37, 38;
exhaustiveness: 9, 43, 48, 49, 50, 52,
  55, 56, 71;
  non-, 43, 44
expansion:
  q-expansion, 37;
  r-expansion, 44
explicandum, 2
explicans, 2, 5, 6, 124
explication, 2, 124